MIRROR IMAGES

For Janice
Inspiring teacher, counselor, and principal
Loving mother, wife, and grandmother

MIRROR IMAGES

New Reflections on Teacher Leadership

CASEY REASON / CLAIR REASON

FOR INFORMATION:

Corwin
A SAGE Company
2455 Teller Road
Thousand Oaks, California 91320
(800) 233–9936
Fax: (800) 417–2466
www.corwin.com

SAGE Ltd.
1 Oliver's Yard
55 City Road
London, EC1Y 1SP
United Kingdom

SAGE India Pvt. Ltd.
B 1/I 1 Mohan Cooperative Industrial Area
Mathura Road, New Delhi 110 044
India

SAGE Asia-Pacific Pte. Ltd.
33 Pekin Street #02–01
Far East Square
Singapore 048763

Acquisitions Editor: Arnis Burvikovs
Associate Editor: Desirée A. Bartlett
Editorial Assistant: Kimberly Greenberg
Production Editor: Amy Schroller
Copy Editor: Taryn Bigelow
Typesetter: Hurix Systems
Proofreader: Victoria Reed-Castro
Indexer: Sylvia Coates
Cover Designer: Anthony Paular
Permissions Editor: Karen Ehrmann

Printed in the United States of America.

Library of Congress Cataloging-in-Publication Data

Reason, Casey S.
Mirror images : new reflections on teacher leadership / Casey Reason, Clair Reason.
p. cm.
Includes bibliographical references and index.
ISBN 978-1-4129-9404-0 (pbk.)
1. Teachers—Professional relationships. 2. Teacher participation in administration. 3. Educational leadership. I. Reason, Clair. II. Title.

LB1775.R34 2011
371.1—dc23

2011029247

This book is printed on acid-free paper.

11 12 13 14 15 10 9 8 7 6 5 4 3 2 1

Contents

Preface

The Purpose

The purpose of this book is to support and empower teachers. By taking a comprehensive look at some new and empowering images of teacher leadership, we hope this text reveals the unique and profound opportunities teachers have today to inspire transformative change in the classroom and beyond. While we seek to inspire you with clear images of what teacher leadership can mean, we also have provided numerous Monday-morning-ready strategies and action steps in each chapter. These will help you not only understand what it means to be a teacher leader today, but will support you in your transformation. We hope this effort is a shared one and that you and teaching colleagues from down the hall and around the world can work together to redefine what teacher leadership can mean for your professional journey and the future prospects of our profession.

The Mirror

You most likely remember the morning before your first day on the job as a teacher. As you zipped, buttoned, and straightened your clothes, you may have looked in the mirror and tried to envision yourself as a teacher. Your brain conjured up images of teachers you'd known and images of teachers from movies and literature. You reflected on the new teacher in the mirror and how he or she would "look" in the classroom.

It is no secret that our actions are driven by the visions we have of ourselves. A new lawyer may visualize him- or herself trying the case of the decade. A local pianist may see him- or herself playing to a sold-out crowd at Carnegie Hall. Our advancement in our chosen profession is driven by these images we carry with us for what we hope to become. The pursuit of this vision is driven by what we see in the mirror and what we believe will someday be staring back at us.

We use the image of the mirror throughout this book because we believe the teaching profession has been flooded with negative, disempowering images of what we do and who we are. We believe our work is heroic and transformative. Yet there are so many images of teaching that portray our journey as pedestrian and dull. Teachers themselves are often characterized as pedantic and uninspiring.

We hope new generations of teachers will look in the mirror each morning with a renewed sense of what's possible in teaching. We hope they see a dynamic teacher leader capable of leading transformation for their students, their school, their community, and the world. For teachers to see these new images, we must do a better job of creating a vision for what it means to be a teacher leader in schools. This book seeks to provide that vision.

Old Reflections, Definitions, and Misconceptions of Teacher Leadership

Many people believe teacher leadership in school is demonstrated by quasi-administrative behaviors. Through the decades, we have known numerous well-intentioned, high-performing teachers who have seen their ascent in the profession limited to providing input in areas in school governance that are more about management than leadership. Rather than developing a meaningful voice in school, these teachers instead find themselves giving input on policy handbooks and building budget allocations. While it certainly takes management to lead, our profession has summarily underused the thoughtful creativity of veteran teachers.

A second misconception involves the difference between teacher leadership and delegated leadership. In many schools, the principal is an excellent delegator. He or she may carefully choose some of the most talented teachers on the staff to execute certain tasks or projects. Thus, teacher leadership has often been seen as the development of highly skilled, "go-to" delegates.

The advancement of teacher leadership should go beyond this model and put teachers at the center of the change process. This enables teachers to help construct a vision, establish a plan for change, and then own the implementation of the change as well as the results. We aren't against delegation. We advocate an evolved notion of what is possible when teachers are given the chance to lead change.

Current Academic Definitions

The literature is replete with definitions of teacher leadership. In 2002, for example, Crowther, Kaagan, Ferguson, and Hann described teacher leadership as an "action that transforms teaching and learning in a school, and ties school and community together on behalf of learning, and that advances social sustainability and quality of life for a community" (p. xvii).

Patterson and Patterson (2004) said that teacher leaders are identified as those who collaborate with colleagues with the intent of improving teaching and learning in both a formal and informal capacity. Teacher leadership has also been defined as "the building of capacity to transform schooling" (Lieberman & Miller, 2005, p. 153) and "the leadership role from one individual to a community of professionals committed to improved student learning" (Katzenmeyer & Moller, 2001, p. 2).

Scholars have noted that teacher leaders are "committed to continuous learning for themselves and their colleagues . . . use systems thinking as a tool to examine complex organizational problems . . . and work toward reconstructing their teaching practices to include roles as servant leaders and change agents in their organizations" (Childs, 2005, pp. 25–26).

Each of these definitions has certainly helped bring us to this point. As such, *Mirror Images: New Reflections on Teacher Leadership* is built on the work of our predecessors. The book is our effort to shed light on what is possible with the advancement of teacher leadership as a mechanism to transform the profession.

New Reflections and Mental Images

In recent years, we have learned that constructing a mental image or vision is a complex, neurological exercise. The visions in our head are shaped by our history, our mental models, and the context from which we work (Reason, 2010). Based on the latest research, we seek nothing less in this book than to construct a new vision of teacher leadership.

To assist in this effort, we have created ten new mental images to represent ten types of teacher leaders. In the chapters that follow, we will elaborate the ten types and discuss their origins and applications. Each type of teacher leader is illustrated with its own icon, or symbol. We did this because teacher leadership can appear to be squishy, theoretical, and amorphous. We hope these symbolic representations will help you to quickly conceptualize each of these visions of teacher leaders and turn those images into actions.

The Learning Advocate: Learning Advocates are teacher leaders whose actions and priorities revolve around one ultimate mission: learning.

The Believer: These passionate teacher leaders believe in their students, colleagues, parents, and the community. They also believe in the lofty aspirations of their profession and are proud of the fact that they teach.

The Transformationalist: The Transformationalist is a teacher leader with an acute capacity to visualize, articulate, and then implement an ambitious, inspiring, and transformative vision for change.

The Synergizer: The Synergizer's gifts involve the capacity to develop and nurture professional networks of support and influence both locally and beyond.

The Method Master: The Method Master is exceptional in the art and science of selecting, learning, and applying research-based, best-practice instructional methods.

The Fully Invested Owner: Fully Invested Owners aren't dabbling in teaching; they are all in. They are invested in "their" students, "their" colleagues, and "their" school.

The Present Balance Keeper: These teacher leaders understand the concept of time better than most and they know that investments in themselves will allow them to serve others more effectively and for a longer period of time.

The Servant: The Servant is a teacher who leads by supporting and developing others.

The Inquisitor: Inquisitors are teacher leaders who inspire their students, their colleagues, and themselves with thoughtful, strategic, purposeful, and emotionally bound questions.

The Detective: Teacher leaders as Detectives solve mysteries and notice things that the untrained eye can't see. These sleuths spot untapped creativity and potential in their students and colleagues alike and help bring forth and nurture those hidden talents.

Perfect Timing or a Perfect Storm?

Teacher leadership is a concept that many of us have embraced for some time. In this section, we present six current trends in education and discuss the degree to which teacher leadership will be important in responding to these shifts. While the argument can be made that teacher leadership has always been important, there are certainly a number of trends emerging today that make the establishment of teacher leadership more important than ever!

Trend #1: Greater Levels of Complexity in the Profession

Our classrooms are more heterogeneous than ever before (George, 2005). This means that our teachers and students come to school with greater dissimilarity in their personal experiences, cultural context, and language. Greater diversity will ultimately result in an improved learning environment. Moving away from a homogeneous perspective is a challenge for many schools and the complexity of dealing with this evolution will certainly require leadership. It will also test our capacity to change at the granular level; and it will be important that teachers themselves are at the heart of this change.

Trend #2: Continued Focus on Accountability and Results

As the era of accountability evolves, teachers will increasingly be required to own their results. To do that, teacher leaders must take part in constructing the vision and establishing an action plan to achieve new outcomes (Leithwood, 1995). Teacher leadership is a perfect approach to create these deeper levels of ownership and accountability.

Trend #3: The Overwhelming Trend Toward Personalization

Technology has allowed us to personalize our lives in unique ways. We can get our news from sources that match our beliefs. Our computer desktops and the cell phones in our pockets allow us to make personal our learning and communication spaces. In a culture that involves high levels of personalization, we are sure to be more resistant to change that is top-down and doesn't consider personal thoughts and ideas.

It has long been acknowledged that leaders are more successful when they can connect on an individual level with those who represent an integral part of the change process. In a culture where we have higher expectations for personalization and involvement, the need for teacher leaders will be greater than ever as we will grow to expect them to either lead the change themselves or be instrumentally involved with whatever changes are necessary in leading schools.

Trend #4: Embarking on the Age of Learning

In an age of information where bodies of knowledge grow exponentially every year, our culture will become increasingly focused on learning capacity and opportunities (Bonk, 2009). The future will bring both accelerated learning expectations and a greater need to develop the capacity to learn in a variety of places and modalities. Lifelong learning will be nonnegotiable and our ability to adapt and continue to learn will arguably be just as important as any learning we have gained up to that point.

Who better to lead the way in an era of learning than teacher leaders?

Trend #5: The Influence of Networks and Open Sourcing

As teachers become more adept at networking, it is likely that national and international cohorts of teachers who serve students at similar points in their development will come together to share ideas, resources, and key innovations. In business and the world of software development, they refer to this practice as open sourcing, wherein challenges or problems are shared in an open "space" and innovations and solutions are offered and debated with fellow professionals. With technology today, those connections could be made down the hall or across the world. The influence of networks and open sourcing will help the teaching profession to continue to evolve in an organic fashion with teachers leading the way thanks to collaboration.

Trend #6: The Emerging Learning Needs of Teachers Who Are Digital Natives

Increasingly, P–12 education will be dominated by teachers who, by one definition or another, are digital natives. Fewer and fewer of us will have grown up without handheld devices and the Internet as constant companions.

People who have grown up with digital sensibilities face innovation and the challenges of change with a much different perspective on solutions than their predecessors. Digital natives are highly collaborative and willing to get input from multiple sources when making a decision. They don't toil away in isolation and are willing to use technology to manage laborious tasks, freeing them to provide interventions at critical learning points.

The emergence of digital natives has created somewhat of a chasm between those who grew up digital and those who didn't. Leaders in schools today can certainly feel this disconnect and the challenges that are created as a result. Teacher leadership will be important in helping these diverse populations work together effectively as they learn from one another and reflect on best practices and approaches from both the digital-native and digital-immigrant perspectives.

Organization and Application of the Book

This book was designed with the busy working professional in mind. We have created simple and clear symbolic representations that we hope will help you remember the content. Each chapter begins with a brief, focused definition of one teacher leader type. We cover the rationale and advantages of each model early in each chapter and then address the specific challenges teacher leaders face when they promote this image of teacher leadership.

Each chapter ends with clear and actionable steps to take to promote and implement this type of teacher leadership in your school and within your own professional practice. Included are steps you can take on your own, as well as ideas you and your colleagues may embrace to make an evolved notion of teacher leadership a significant part of your professional lives.

Acknowledgments

The authors of this book wish to thank the Metro Detroit Galileo Leadership Consortium for their years of service and scholarship in the area of teacher leadership. Several of the teacher leaders featured in this text were graduates of this consortium and their heroic work in the classroom was no doubt inspired by the collegial spirit and guidance they received by being part of Galileo.

The authors of this book were both trained at the University of Toledo and Bowling Green State University, two outstanding academic institutions that helped to formulate our views today.

Our greatest influence for this work was decades of service working with teachers throughout Ohio and Michigan. Our teaching colleagues in Findlay, Oregon, and Sylvania, Ohio, and our colleagues in Petersburg, Lincoln Consolidated, and Northville, Michigan, provided us with a multitude of invaluable insights into the teaching profession. They showed us what is possible with vision, dedication, and desire.

Finally, we wish to thank all of you who are new to the profession or are training to become teachers. Thank you for making this honorable choice. We hope this book can inspire you to move beyond the previous limits of what is possible—for your students, for the profession, and for yourselves.

Publisher's Acknowledgments

Corwin would like to thank the following individuals for taking the time to provide their editorial insight:

Mary Johnstone, Principal
Rabbit Creek Elementary School
Anchorage, AK

Toni Jones, Chief Academic Officer
Deer Creek Public Schools
Edmond, OK

Kylie Lake, Primary Teacher
Specialist for literacy, math, and social emotional learning
Rabbit Creek Elementary
Anchorage, AK

Alice L. Manus, Assistant Principal Curriculum & Instruction
Soldan International Studies High School
St. Louis, MO

Melanie Mares Sainz, Academic Coach
Lowndes Middle School
Valdosta, GA

About the Authors

Casey Reason (right) and Clair "Tuffy" Reason

Casey Reason is a writer, researcher, and consultant who has worked with international thought leaders on breakthrough strategies designed to improve performance and overcome resistance to change. Dr. Reason's approaches are founded on the emerging body of research in brain science and adult learning theory. Casey's work as an instructional designer was prominently featured in a Forbes.com article in 2010 and he has been a featured speaker in conferences all over the world for the past ten years. Casey is a former high school principal and assistant superintendent. His book, *Leading a Learning Organization: The Science of Working With Others* was released in January of 2010 and was selected by Phi Delta Kappa International to be a 2010 PDK Book Club selection. Dr. Reason lives in Scottsdale, Arizona, with his twin sons, Brice and Kiah.

Clair "Tuffy" Reason attended the University of Toledo, where he received his bachelor's degree in education and was a Mid-American Conference Champion Division I basketball player. In the Army, Tuffy was a member of the Border Patrol in West Germany and served as a reporter for the *Stars and*

Stripes military newspaper. After college and the army, he worked in commercial radio as a sportscaster, news writer, and talk show interviewer at stations in Ohio and Michigan. Tuffy then earned his master's degree in education from Bowling Green State University and taught English and Speech at Clay High School in Oregon, Ohio, for 26 years. He also was a teacher and administrator at Lourdes College in Sylvania, Ohio, and at Bowling Green State University. He, with his wife Janice, lives in Scottsdale, Arizona, where he continues work as a writer, editor, and program planner for Highpoint Learning, Incorporated.

1

Profiles in Teacher Leadership Today

We begin this book with four compelling stories that illustrate what is possible when teachers embrace teacher leadership. What makes these stories so interesting and unique is how dramatically different they are from one another. We hope these stories will show you that your journey in teacher leadership is your own, and the evolution of how you see yourself—that image in the mirror—is driven by the choices you make. Read the following stories carefully. We speak of them repeatedly throughout the book as authentic examples of each concept in action. Don't become just a "mirror image" of teachers you have seen in the past. Instead, embrace your own vision for what is possible and create the type of teacher leader you are destined to be.

She Changed Their Lives and Found Herself

Kate Murray is an English and French teacher and department chair for her high school in a wealthy suburb near Detroit.

Historically, Detroit has been one of the most segregated metro areas in the United States and Kate teaches in a predominately Caucasian, wealthy, and high-performing high school. Students who attend the school come from affluent families. Many of these families made their money as top executives in the auto industry.

Kate's school has gone through a rather dramatic change in the last several years. Confronting a shrinking urban population, numerous high schools in the city of Detroit were shut down almost overnight. Students from these schools were rerouted to every corner of the city and some found themselves redistricted altogether, suddenly in the mix with these wealthy suburbs.

Following multiple generations of homogenous, high achievement, Kate's high school faced a unique challenge—assimilating a small but significant number of African American students whose culture, background, and educational opportunities had been anything but equal. Suddenly without a school, the students were asked to connect with a building unfamiliar to them in every way possible.

Not surprisingly, these new students struggled in every way. Many had extremely low reading scores and would by all accounts be considered at risk or low performing. While Kate's school welcomed these new students, it was undoubtedly a difficult challenge for everyone to be faced with supporting students whose culture, background, and academic challenges were very different from the students they had served in the past.

Like many of her colleagues, Kate experienced some disconnect given her experience as a teacher in an affluent building. She also had a personal disconnect as she had gone to high school in a wealthy Chicago suburb and attended a prestigious college. As a young, white woman with this pedigree, Kate knew how hard it would be to connect with these students in a way that would best meet their needs. Kate also knew that she was thinking of leaving teaching. As she thought about her future, she wondered if her "image" of a teacher wasn't more appropriately linked to a pursuit of higher education and perhaps a career as an Ivy League professor. Kate was at a crossroads.

When she entered teaching, Kate had responded to what you may know as "the calling." While she could count many victories in the classroom and had served her students well in her short career, Kate realized that the challenge in front of her was transcendent—and one she couldn't ignore. She realized these students were in trouble. If her high school didn't respond appropriately, it was likely these students would drop out and face numerous economic and social challenges.

Kate began with the academic challenges these students faced in reading and writing. She organized a program called Freshman Assist, designed to help transitioning ninth graders boost their reading levels and develop study skills in preparation for a new, competitive environment. Kate approached her department's reading teacher about teaching in the Freshman Assist program. She refused the assignment. Placing visions of graduate school and a doctoral thesis on hold, Kate ignored convention and took on the challenge herself.

At this point, almost everyone thought Kate was in over her head. She had never taught reading and she knew her students' academic deficits were excruciatingly difficult. She admitted that she didn't know or understand their culture and would have to make a commitment to improve her knowledge in this area. Not to be deterred, Kate worked hard to become the loving and supportive guide she hoped to be for those students.

Naysayers said Kate was out of her element. She was the wrong color, had the wrong background, and wasn't academically prepared for the job she was trying to do. After all, many of these students had reading scores at the second- or third-grade level. The prospect of getting these unacquainted, uncomfortable, and academically challenged students through the ninth grade and in a position to graduate was a challenge that few at the school actually thought Kate could meet.

What these pessimists didn't know about Kate, and perhaps what she didn't know about herself, was that she was a fighter. She decided to pursue additional academic credentials in reading and literacy and immersed herself in literature related to working with students from tough, economically disadvantaged backgrounds. The more she read, the more excited she became about the opportunity to transform the lives of the students she served.

Much to everyone's surprise, one year after Kate's homemade program began, each of the troubled, academically challenged students was reading at grade level. In addition to raising their reading scores, Kate had also become their leader and guide. They came to her when they faced challenges in other classes and she encouraged them. She raised expectations and supported each of them in meeting her demands.

Suffice to say, Kate's success caught the attention of her principal and the school board. They elected to continue support for the program. Kate reshaped the program into what is known today as FAST, the Freshman Academic Success Team. This evolution identified other subject-matter teachers who understood her mission and were willing to help this special group of students. These teachers joined forces with the goal of saving the students.

With new levels of support, the second cohort of students in the FAST program saw an amazing turnaround in their reading scores, as well as in their academic readiness in other core subject areas. The relationships they established with the teachers helped the displaced high school students feel wanted and appreciated. For the teachers involved, the admiration was mutual.

When the students left Kate's program, she remained connected to them. She supported them throughout their high school years. Astonishingly, all of the students in Kate's first year of the program graduated on time and attended college. Today, Kate can reflect on her first freshman group with pride. She shared her passion, set the bar high, and helped each student achieve unexpected results through discipline, connection, love, and consistency.

Kate is a hero in the hearts of the students she serves. When she heard her calling as a teacher, she embraced the challenge and found the unique treasures waiting to emerge from her students, her colleagues, and herself. She became a teacher leader who reshaped her own image of what it means to lead, teach, learn, and grow.

* * *

They Learned to Live the Lesson

Several years ago, Khris Nedam's sixth-grade class in Northville, Michigan, read Robert Coles' *The Story of Ruby Bridges.* The book is about a four-year-old African American girl who made national headlines as one of the first black children to break the educational color barrier in Louisiana. They also read Marshall Poe's *Little Rock Nine,* a similar story about black high school students in Arkansas. Khris's students were moved by the struggles these students faced just to get an education. They reflected aloud with Khris on how fortunate they were to live in a community where education was available to everyone.

Later, while these same students studied twentieth-century segregation, they were shocked to learn that in many regions of Afghanistan girls were not allowed an education. The brutal rule of the Taliban made change and progress difficult. In what might be described as the ultimate teachable moment, the students looked at Khris and asked, "Is there anything we can do to make this better?"

If you were to observe Khris in her classroom, you might describe her as a "typical" Michigan elementary teacher. Khris, however, is anything but average. She is unusually intelligent and has spent a lifetime serving the needs of others. She has traveled internationally many times, traversing rugged terrain to help those who might otherwise never be served.

Her journeys brought her satisfaction in service, as well as the knowledge that providing this type of help is not for the faint of heart. Khris knew that to teach her students what it takes to make a difference, they would have to understand that profound action and sacrifice would be required. While most of us would feel good if we held a fund-raiser and sent a check, Khris and her students shocked the world when they announced plans to build a school in Wonkhai, Afghanistan.

Few beyond Khris, her professional network, and her students believed this was anything but a dream. Most teachers, parents, and community members thought the pursuit absurd. The reality would involve changing tribal paradigms in Wonkhai to get approval from the village elders to allow girls to go to school. If the elders approved, they would still have to go to the Taliban leadership to ask their permission. Even if they leaped all these hurdles, Khris and her students would still need to raise a substantial amount of money to support the project.

Anyone who has served on a bond or construction committee in their school district understands how difficult it is to erect a school. Imagine trying to do it halfway around the world with dramatic cultural challenges, hostile political forces, and the economic difficulty of fund-raising and hoping the dollars would be appropriately spent. As you might imagine, not all parents embraced the merits of their sons and daughters giving time, energy, and family treasure to support an effort in Afghanistan.

Khris and her students began their journey to make a difference in 1998. In January of 2001, construction was complete on a six-room schoolhouse complete with many of the accoutrements of a modern school in the United States. In just 36 months, the simple question, "Is there anything we can do to make this better?" was answered in a profound, transformative, and life-changing way.

In 2011, Khris and her Kids 4 Afghan Kids project continue to fund and nurture the enterprise. Over the years, their efforts have led to the construction of two elementary buildings, one secondary school, an orphanage, and a health clinic. They also have an orchard, stables, and livestock as moneymaking resources for extra needs that arise.

Khris has an uncommon spirit and drive. She didn't listen to the monotonous negativity of those who tried to make ugly her students' beautiful acts. Khris showed inspirational ability to influence others with love, generosity, and kindness. And her journey in teacher leadership stands as an exemplar of how to lead change at the most significant levels.

A fifth-grade teacher in an unexceptional classroom, Khris emerged as an exceptional and transcendent school leader. While Khris came into the profession with a unique notion of service and contribution, her impressive actions in connection with this project redefined her vision of herself as a teacher leader. She also raised the bar for all of us, in redefining what is possible in a classroom.

* * *

Her Quiet Diligence

Three decades ago, Mary Ann Nowacki began her education career while teaching in a prison in Cleveland, Ohio. If you met Mary Ann today, you wouldn't be surprised at her ability to deal with the prison environment. Her toughness is unmistakable, yet her compassion and love for teaching are undeniable.

It was at this first job in the prison that she realized the quiet, reserved young woman she was could only emerge as a teacher if she learned to connect with others. The new teacher she saw in the mirror also needed a certain toughness she hadn't discovered. Mary Ann's tenure as a teacher in the prison helped her acquire a thoughtful confidence that would serve her well in the decades to come.

After leaving the prison job in Cleveland, Mary Ann was hired at the biggest high school in Ohio. She joined a department with twenty veteran math teachers who had the strength and confidence needed to survive in a large, urban setting. Working in this environment represented yet another challenge for Mary Ann. She was still new to teaching and students and teachers alike have a tendency to get lost in these large environments. Mary Ann knew she would have to be special to make her mark with colleagues and learners. While there are many ways to stand out in a crowd, Mary Ann decided to distinguish herself by becoming an amazing classroom teacher.

Mary Ann buckled down and honed her craft. Year after year, she adopted new strategies to connect with her students. Her colleagues began to notice her energy, passion, and dedication. Her high school had an active teachers' association and union leadership encouraged Mary Ann to serve on various association subcommittees. She was an ideal choice because she was young, energetic, and increasingly confident. Furthermore, she loved her profession and didn't mind advocating for the teaching colleagues she was growing to care about more with each passing year.

The teachers' association gleefully used her as their voice during difficult moments because of her outstanding reputation. It was impossible for detractors to claim that Mary Ann's union advocacy was based on laziness or a desire to simply coast. Everyone knew about the long hours she worked and her unbelievable diligence in the classroom. When she spoke out for the union, it was impossible not to listen. Mary Ann realized that her diligence and dedication to her craft had allowed her to succeed in ways she hadn't imagined.

Many teachers would have been satisfied with this image of excellence in the mirror each morning. But not Mary Ann. Her efforts to search out new instructional practices were never-ending. At the time, the idea of cooperative learning was surging in popularity. Mary Ann decided to get some training in this approach; she was hooked after day one.

Mary Ann became an impassioned advocate for cooperative learning and began researching everything she could find on the subject. For her, this model created energy, connection, and focus in her classroom and allowed her to strategically differentiate instruction without halting progress for the rest of the class. It gave her students a chance to lead, learn together, collaborate, and develop skills they would need as adults.

Colleagues who did not know Mary Ann very well looked at her endeavors and said, "There's no way you can use cooperative learning for every class, every day.

It's impossible." Winking and smiling, Mary Ann replied, "Oh yes you can. Come by my room any day of the week, any week of the year. You'll see." Her determination and conviction were hard to resist.

Mary Ann's reputation as an outstanding instructor made everything she said important to her teaching colleagues. Her failure rates were extremely low and students in her class showed a unique affection for math, their classmates, and Mary Ann. Soon, she became the local expert in cooperative learning. Then, teachers throughout the Toledo area saw Mary Ann as the regional expert in cooperative learning and she happily gave her time to help teaching colleagues learn what she knew.

Mary Ann eventually developed a statewide reputation for classroom excellence. She spoke at state conferences and shared as much expertise as her energies allowed. As Mary Ann's expertise increased, she could have launched a website, written a book, and made a reputation in the industry as a high-powered consultant. Instead, Mary Ann kept her focus where she wanted it: in the classroom. Her life's work was to ignite her students' passion for math and to help them strive toward excellence.

Mary Ann knew that her highest achievement as a teacher wouldn't result in a standing ovation at a conference or a publisher's report on book sales. She was wise enough to know that it would come in quiet moments when she knew her efforts had made a difference in her students' lives. For a teacher leader, this is professional satisfaction at its best.

One afternoon as Mary Ann was busy in her classroom, she noticed a well-dressed young man standing in the doorway. It was Donte, one of the most difficult students the school had ever known. After multiple suspensions and what seemed like an inability to get along with any teacher, it appeared he might become another dropout statistic in a large, urban area.

When he joined Mary Ann's class, she, too, experienced his challenging ways. He struggled with the content. He did everything he could to disrupt his classmates and his teacher.

But thanks to Mary Ann's wit, grit, and strategy, Donte survived the year in Mary Ann's class. In fact, he had unusual success working with her. It was not surprising, then, that Donte was placed in her class for his sophomore year.

After two years with Mary Ann, Donte had discovered that he could be successful academically and that he could get along with his teachers. On his last day with her, Mary Ann wished Donte well and watched as he disappeared into the vast sea that was her high school. She had not spoken to Donte since, so Mary Ann was shocked to see him back at her door.

"Donte! Welcome back!" Mary Ann said with a smile. With a look of shock, Donte replied, "You remember me?" In her sly teacher voice, Mary Ann said with a wink, "Now, Donte. How could I forget you?" Donte looked at the class of students in front of him. He probably saw himself in a few of their faces.

Donte had been a loud, wisecracking student who always took the joke too far. He had been a constant distraction to those around him and his actions made him difficult to work with. Now, to Mary Ann's surprise, Donte's voice was sweet, quiet, and humble. Donte said, "I came back to see you, Mrs. Nowacki. I wanted to tell you that I never would have made it through high school without you. You believed in me and you didn't give up."

Mary Ann hugged Donte before he left the room in an emotional moment between a teacher leader and a student she loved. There were tears in her eyes as Donte thanked her again and walked out the door.

At the end of the hour, Mary Ann's class had moved on and she was busy grading papers in the solitude of her room. A smile came across her face as she thought about Donte and how far he had come. No placard was issued and no lengthy soliloquy was delivered. She didn't get a raise in pay, but in that moment of solitude, Mary Ann experienced the most profound satisfaction that a teacher leader can have. She knew that her teaching had made a difference in the life of a student. She knew that not every student would come back to thank her, but the confirmation she had received from Donte was what this teacher leader had been searching for.

* * *

The Master Motivator

When Jim Mayzes became a physical education teacher, he brought optimism, fitness, and focus to his job. He had worked as a manager in one of the largest health clubs in the city but decided that his true calling wasn't going to be measured in the number of sales he generated or the amount of money he made. Instead, he decided, teaching physical education and coaching football would be his destiny.

When Jim was named the high school football coach, he experienced an unforgettable greeting in the teachers' lounge. Renee, a fellow gym teacher, chirped loudly in front of the room, "Hey, Jim! Did you really take the head football coaching job?" With a quick smile, Jim said, "Yes I did, Renee." She went on, "You should have waited for the golf coaching job to open up. This school has never won a league championship in football and never will." Although her statement wasn't all that funny, the lounge exploded with laughter. Several of the staff's most disconnected teachers were particularly appreciative of Renee's attack. Jim just smiled. "We'll see."

Despite the inappropriateness of Renee's caustic attack, there was good reason to be skeptical of Jim's capacity to be successful in the position. Their town had never embraced football and the school's team had never won more than six games in a ten-game season.

There were many theories as to why the team had never been very good. Some said the community had too many wealthy parents who weren't tough enough to get their sons and daughters to compete. Others chalked it up to several decades of poor performance and an inability to adjust expectations. A number of talented athletes were lured away from Jim's public school and went instead to highly competitive private high schools. To some, Jim's first coaching job didn't seem like a very good opportunity because there appeared to be so many factors working against him.

Jim's fire, optimism, hard work, and dedication were evident from the first moment of his first season. Local fans noticed a significant change in the intensity of the players. Each week, the team became a more competitive adversary. Going into the tenth and last game of the season, Jim's team had already won six games. They had tied the team's record for the most number of wins in a season. But Jim and his team weren't satisfied. They thought that winning that seventh game would put them in a special category and would explode the myths about what was possible for their football team.

That tenth game, however, was being played on the road against a team that was unbeaten in nine games and was counting on one last win to vault them into the state playoffs. It was a cold, rainy midwestern fall night. Jim's team was outmatched and observers in the know were predicting a blowout. After three and a half quarters of play, however, there was no blowout. Jim's team had fought fiercely and, heading into the last half of the fourth quarter, was only down by a few points. But Jim's players did even better than that. With just a few minutes to go, they took the lead by four.

This great moment was short-lived, however, as the championship team was not to be denied. Powered by one of the top offenses in the state, the home team's quarterback drove the team downfield and with a minute remaining, was only a yard away from scoring the winning touchdown.

Jim's fans in the bleachers were heartbroken. The team had fought so hard, but at this point it seemed inevitable that they would lose in the final minute of play. Jim, however, wasn't finished yet. With rain dripping off his hat, Jim ran onto the field and implored his players to stand their ground, fill their gaps, and prevent an enormous push on the part of the offense.

On both the first and second downs, the running back crashed into the line and tried to drive into the end zone. Despite being smaller than their opponents, Jim's team fought with tenacity and held their ground. On the third down, the offense again pushed toward the goal line only to be stopped in their tracks.

Exhausted, covered in mud, and having pushed themselves to the limit, team members huddled for their final time out. Jim asked his team to hold their ground one last time. The final snap came almost in slow motion. The quarterback rolled to the left and dove for the end zone. The defense met him head on and drove him into the backfield.

The game was over. Jim's team had won their seventh game of the season against an undefeated team, broken the record for most wins in a season in the history of the school, and proven what is possible with motivation, energy, belief, and passion.

It was tempting for Jim to go back to Renee and the others and say, "I told you so!" Instead, Jim spent the next seventeen years continuing to transform the program. His teams won the league title eleven times, were undefeated during the regular season twice, became regional champions twice, and appeared in the state championship twice, winning it all in 2008.

Jim's passion as a teacher leader helped transform his team, his school, and his community. Jim has spent a generation building an example of what is possible when you believe. As Jim looked in the mirror as he readied himself to teach and coach each day, he was the only one who saw the future that would unfold for him and his students. Certainly, that image of teacher leadership is now recognizable to everyone.

2

The Learning Advocate

Learning is a treasure that will follow its owner everywhere.
—Chinese Proverb

The Learning Advocate Defined

Learning Advocates are teacher leaders whose actions and priorities revolve around one ultimate mission: learning. They are always working toward the continuous improvement of learning conditions in their school. They seek to maximize learning for their students and they make decisions that impact student learning. They seek to create ideal learning conditions for the adults who work in their school. They acknowledge that their individual and collective success as educators will be driven primarily by their ability to learn. The Learning Advocate's passion for learning is contagious and these teacher leaders help each of us learn more, do more, and ultimately become more.

Why We Need the Learning Advocate

Being a Learning Advocate as a teacher leader seems like an all-too-simple starting point. After all, isn't learning at the heart of what it means to be a teacher? Isn't learning advocacy an obvious aspect of the job?

Sadly, those of us who have been in the profession for decades know that the focus on learning is often either missing or is lost along the way. New board members will be elected and often find, to their surprise, that making decisions that impact learning is one of the last things they are asked to accomplish. Superintendents, principals, and curriculum directors are often so bogged down in the minutiae of their daily work that they readily admit they have precious little time to devote to the all-important objective of being an instructional leader. Even teachers find themselves so caught up in the grind of "teaching" that they are left with few opportunities to reflect upon or advocate for learning.

Leaders at every level must find themselves more consistently engaged in deep, meaningful dialogue about learning. This requires the support of parents, politicians, principals, and the central office. But the most important learning advocacy must come from the front line—the teachers themselves.

The Learning Advocate: Advantages and Benefits

They Bring Their Knowledge of Learning to the Classroom and Support Enhanced Learning in Their School

Teacher leaders who are Learning Advocates understand that learning is both an art and a science (Reason, 2010). While teachers have an unending list of priorities, teacher leaders who are Learning Advocates realize that no matter how chaotic their school life becomes, they must consistently search for new knowledge related to learning and attempt to apply this knowledge whenever possible.

When Learning Advocates embrace this concept and focus their attention on stimulating learning, students become more engaged, their learning improves, and the opportunity for significant improvements in student achievement increases.

They Stimulate Deep Learning Throughout the School and Support Breakthrough Thinking

Learning Advocates focus on factors that stimulate their learning and the learning of their students. They are outstanding contributors to the school improvement process. Their presence helps create the focus and energy necessary for using the ever-increasing knowledge regarding learning and reflecting on what this new knowledge can mean for creating change. Learning Advocates become the ultimate catalysts for change. They are always helping others to learn more and to promote the best school improvement strategies and approaches.

They Help Others Focus on the Bigger Picture During Times of Change

Teacher leaders operating as Learning Advocates often are conduits to a calmer and more focused team-learning environment. Local battles regarding turf, tradition, and a myriad of other short-term challenges are never as important to the Learning Advocate as the long-term objective of creating a more effective learning environment.

Losing the battle over a preferred textbook doesn't mean the end of progress. Instructional approaches, curriculum, textbooks, technology, and schedules are all tools we will continue to change and improve upon as long as we work in the profession. The Learning Advocate never loses sight of the fact that, in the end, learning is the real prize.

Short-term attempts to raise student achievement scores or address a particularly inflamed, localized need may cause stress for everyone involved. Maintaining a longer-term focus on learning offers an increased sense of purpose among the teachers who adopt this mind-set. When the Learning Advocate is able to reduce stress and bring a greater sense of calm to the learning environment, the school itself accomplishes more.

Studies show a reduction in fear and stress results in improved learning opportunities (Compton, 2003; Pekrun, Maier, & Elliot, 2009). The deepest levels of learning always emerge in calm and relaxed environments (Caine, Caine, McClintic, & Klimek, 2005). Teacher leaders who are Learning Advocates are great models for this calmer, more relaxed atmosphere.

They Promote Better Policy, Smarter Governance, and Advocate for the Right Strategies for Change

Teacher leaders who are Learning Advocates see change in terms of its impact on learning. Unfortunately, it's easy to get distracted from this priority. Many schools immerse themselves in a plan for change that revolves around some adjustment to the daily schedule. When these changes are considered, many of the conversations focus on how this affects the adults in the school rather than the students and their learning. When adopting a new textbook, teams of leaders often lose themselves in evaluating their own preferences rather than reflecting on how the use of the material will impact student learning.

Schools also forget about learning when attempting to resolve governance and managerial issues. For example, a building practice wherein students are interrupted in class to resolve an issue like tardiness or an overdue library book may solve nagging problems. But what toll does this take on learning?

It's easy to be critical and blame the profession for being shortsighted in making decisions that are good for the moment, but bad in the long run. Keep in mind that we are just now beginning to scratch the surface in what we know about learning. We have established practices in the past based on relatively little knowledge about the intricacies of the learning process. Thus, the Learning Advocate steers us away from decisions made in response to paradigms from the past and instead moves us toward an enlightened perspective focused on elements of change that benefit learning.

Looking in the Mirror: Becoming the Learning Advocate

There are many advantages for teacher leaders operating as Learning Advocates. Like so many aspects of school improvement, our systems often struggle to implement change even when it seems logical. This is due to the images of our profession that we carry in our individual and collective brains and how we are supposed to operate within it.

In this section and those that follow in subsequent chapters, we will help you conceptualize each type of teacher leadership by juxtaposing these new visions with long-held, previously established precepts you have likely encountered in your career. Reinventing what it means to be a teacher means changing these old images. In the tables that follow (see pp. 20 and 21), the list on the left presents "old reflections." The list on the right shows the corresponding "new reflections" you need to conceptualize to become a Learning Advocate.

This list provides a Likert-type scale wherein you will be asked to choose a score between zero and five in one of two directions. We ask that you look at this list and evaluate where you fall between the old and new reflections. You are encouraged to ensure that your perception reflects your work in the classroom.

This scale is not designed to embarrass or degrade. Instead, it is constructed to call out those existing paradigms and beliefs that will be helpful for you later in the chapter when we outline some actions you can take to become a teacher leader as Learning Advocate.

Discussion of Classroom Applications

Checking the list on the left, we can trace a number of formative reasons why schools tend to work in the way we have described. Numerous management issues that stemmed from larger schools being formed through consolidation in the early

Classroom Applications for the Learning Advocate

Old Reflection		*New Reflection*
Learning is a mystery: I follow my intuition.	5 4 3 2 1 0 1 2 3 4 5 ◄──►	Learning is a science: I follow the research.
My teaching is the focus in my classroom.	5 4 3 2 1 0 1 2 3 4 5 ◄──►	Student learning is the focus in my classroom.
My classroom environment focuses on control.	5 4 3 2 1 0 1 2 3 4 5 ◄──►	My classroom environment focuses on stimulating deep levels of engagement.
My learning plan is set and I rarely deviate from my plan.	5 4 3 2 1 0 1 2 3 4 5 ◄──►	My learning plan is set, but I deviate constantly based on the learning needs of my students.
Students attempt to learn what I am ready to teach.	5 4 3 2 1 0 1 2 3 4 5 ◄──►	I teach what the students are ready to learn.

twentieth century led to habits, priorities, and visions for teaching that we still maintain today. We still struggle with making the shift from a focus on management, control, and teaching to a perspective designed to promote learning and personalizing our approaches in the classroom to help students become more engaged.

As you consider the shift away from these old reflections, keep in mind that in your K–12 experiences as a student, you undoubtedly experienced a learning environment where the vision of learning was more aligned with the list on the left than that on the right. When you become a transcendent teacher leader and help schools begin to operate differently, it is important to understand where you came from and where you still hope to go. This will be an important step in embracing and enhancing learning advocacy.

Schoolwide Change for the Learning Advocate

Old Reflection		*New Reflection*
The principal or central office determines teacher learning needs.	5 4 3 2 1 0 1 2 3 4 5 ⟷	Teacher learning needs are revealed by their collective work in the classroom.
Teacher learning happens on professional development days.	5 4 3 2 1 0 1 2 3 4 5 ⟷	Teacher learning happens every day, everywhere.
Teachers learn alone.	5 4 3 2 1 0 1 2 3 4 5 ⟷	Teachers learn together, alone, online, and face-to-face.
School change revolves around schedules and processes.	5 4 3 2 1 0 1 2 3 4 5 ⟷	School change revolves around new things teachers learn and subsequently apply.
Teachers are collectively judged in the school by how well they teach.	5 4 3 2 1 0 1 2 3 4 5 ⟷	Teachers are collectively judged in the school by how well students learn.

Discussion of Schoolwide Change

Professional development is still a top-down function in many schools. Teachers arrive at training activities with little idea about what they are going to accomplish or how their learning is supposed to be applied in the classroom. Considering what we know about how important it is to establish a basic learning context, even for adults, it is absurd to ask adults to come to training activities without efforts to prepare them for the learning. This is still an all-too-common practice.

In terms of schoolwide change, there still are many schools where teachers continue to work in isolation. This habit of isolation evolved because of managerial practices created generations ago designed to separate workers as a means for establishing and maintaining control (Jones, 2000). Schools in the early 1900s were designed to promote isolation. This kept information from flowing and allowed managers to exert greater control.

Unfortunately, this habit is still prevalent in schools today and it will take generational change to help us rethink what it means to work together in schools. We know, neurologically speaking, that when teachers have the opportunity to collaborate, they are stimulated to a much greater extent and learn that much more (Achterman & Loertscher, 2008; Chapman, Ramondt, & Smiley, 2005). Overcoming our past will be key to building a better future.

Strategies for Becoming and Supporting the Learning Advocate

This chapter has presented you with an inspiring definition of what it means to become the Learning Advocate. We have explored the advantages and benefits teacher leaders bring to classrooms and schools. We have reviewed competing factors preventing us from consistently promoting learning advocacy in our schools.

This section is designed to move the conversation away from the abstract and present specific strategies teacher leaders can use to begin their journey to becoming a Learning Advocate. The strategies suggested below don't have to be done in order. Nor do you have to complete all of the activities to demonstrate progress. Becoming a teacher leader who is a Learning Advocate can only be achieved over time, but by employing some of these strategies, we are confident that you will see immediate benefits.

Learning Study Team Strategy

Since the year 2000, we have learned more about the brain, how it functions, and the steps we can take to stimulate learning than we ever knew before (Bonnema, 2009). This avalanche of new knowledge offers us a number of variables to consider as we evolve in our habits and professional practice and collectively consider how to stimulate the deepest levels of school reform and change.

Because the science of learning is changing so rapidly, teachers today must be avid consumers of research. Then they must reflect on this new knowledge and consider its applications in the classroom and throughout the school. Learning is our collective craft. Time spent studying other issues related to curriculum, assessment, and instructional strategies will matter little if we don't understand what is required to stimulate the human mind.

We recommend that teachers commit to a lifelong study of the science of learning. They should make it their job to be community experts on the topic. Using today's technology, teachers can activate scholarship-oriented search engines to consistently sort through articles and research updates related to learning. They should maintain an active reading agenda and participate in book studies, blogs, and other interactive learning opportunities. We expect dentists, cardiologists, and oncologists to be on the cutting edge of their fields and apply the latest findings to their work. Learning is our business, and we should do the same.

One of the major obstacles we have in remaining current is time. While reading this text, you may recognize a good idea but feel that it is too much to fit in yet another research-and-reading effort in your professional life. This is why learning study teams make sense. If teacher leaders who are Learning Advocates can commit to collaborating and doing small amounts of work periodically, it is easy to come together several times a year, share resources, and stay on top of the ever-changing research base on learning. Put simply, by making the job of staying current a team effort, it becomes simpler and can be more fun and fulfilling.

Learning Implications Strategy

Today, schools are participating in more collaboration and teaming than ever before. Professional learning communities promote the idea that teachers need to establish working groups that meet consistently, engage in meaningful dialogue on professional practice, and develop improved strategies and approaches. We have closely studied how teams work and what we can do to be most effective as team members.

One strategy that works involves establishing specific roles and responsibilities for each team member. For example, it is common to assign a timekeeper for the group. Perhaps another person could be asked to monitor the level of collegial input, ensuring that everyone gets a chance to speak. Another new role to consider is the Learning Advocate. A Learning Advocate on any team of teachers should continually ask, "When are we going to address learning?" or "What are the learning implications of the decision we're making?" This makes learning a priority in staff meetings, departmental discussions, school-improvement planning sessions, or at any other time that learning implications are being considered.

Consistently examining the learning implications of any change will help teams make better decisions. It will improve student achievement and learning outcomes as well. We recommend assigning a Learning Advocate to every team. We often find ourselves caught up in the moment in schools and we lose sight of our cherished priorities. Making this a priority for our meeting times ensures that we address learning in a consistent and strategic way.

Learning for Fun Strategy

The focus on collaboration and learning as professional functions isn't a passing trend. Futurists predict that experts in virtually every profession will have to continue to learn and apply that learning, thoughtfully and strategically (Bonk, 2009). Learning together is here to stay. Thus, it is a great strategy for Learning Advocates to make learning fun. We encourage Learning Advocates to create learning opportunities with a focus on engagement, collegiality, and connection. Of course teams have to do their work. But there is no reason why the journey can't be a rich and exciting adventure.

So when teams come together to learn, don't forget to allow these meetings to be fun. Providing refreshments, building in chances for celebration, and adding humor are all good ideas whenever possible. It sends the message that learning together is something to enjoy, not just a discipline that must be mastered.

If you've ever watched a group of enthusiastic adults at play in a leisure activity, it's clear that as human beings we enjoy connecting with one another and will work extremely hard when we see the outcomes as being fun and enjoyable. All of us at times work harder at play than we do some days at work. Why not engage that natural sensibility and make team learning more fun?

Professional Learning Communities Strategy

The adoption of professional learning communities (PLCs) promotes learning advocacy at the highest levels. One assumption about PLCs is that once you set them up, teachers will have the opportunity to reflect and collaborate in the name of learning (DuFour, Eaker, & DuFour, 2008).

The establishment of PLCs, however, does not guarantee a focus on learning. While schools institute collaborative planning time and build in systemic structures for analyzing data, the key in the next generation of this model will be increased attention and dedication to learning itself.

While teams within a PLC must consistently evaluate their progress based upon student data and their relative levels of improvement, learning advocacy can be advanced if teachers make their own and their team's learning a key component of what it means to work in the PLC. We must constantly ask ourselves, "How well are we learning as a team?" "Are we improving our capacity to learn new things as a result of working together?" and "Does working within this PLC improve our ability to individually reflect and learn new things?"

PLCs give us the vehicle to focus on learning. Making learning advocacy a goal for the group helps move this ideal forward. We recommend that the PLC address the questions above on a regular basis, perhaps quarterly or semiannually as a means for assessing the progress of the group.

Community Learning Expert Strategy

Scholars of teacher leadership feel that as a teacher evolves and matures, he or she has an even greater level of influence in their world (Martin & Shoho, 2000). Teacher leaders as Learning Advocates understand that their expertise in stimulating learning is a wonderful resource to the communities they serve.

These teachers look for places or opportunities to share their knowledge in the community and to increase advocacy and levels of interest. When Learning Advocates share their expertise, they raise the stature of teaching in the community and help to develop a more collaborative school and community culture.

We recommend that Learning Advocates actively work to place themselves in the community, sharing their expertise as often as possible. A school improvement team may make community-learning advocacy a goal, complete with plans and evaluations at certain points in the year. What have we done this year to show the community that we are learning experts?

From a public relations standpoint, it is hard to argue against the notion of putting ourselves out in the community, showing our constituents that to teach today requires very different skills and abilities than in previous generations. Demonstrating this expertise to the public produces a level of professionalism that will reap benefits for the school and everyone involved.

Needs-Based Learning Strategy

When thinking about school improvement, we sometimes make the mistake of assuming that the only way we can learn something new and grow as a staff is to make strategic use of professional development days or training opportunities that are typically built into the annual calendar. This perspective puts enormous pressure on providing the right type of professional development on these important days.

While professional development days are essential, we realize there are a number of spontaneous learning opportunities for teachers and principals to promote professional learning on a consistent basis. Learning for teachers and staff must be seen as both formal and spontaneous.

A key step in making this shift will be to encourage teachers to monitor their own learning agenda and identify through collaboration their areas of need or weakness. Some questions a team could explore at meetings would be, "What are our most pressing learning needs at this time?"and "What new learning do we need to embrace to do a better job in stimulating student learning?" Unfortunately, honest conversations are held far too infrequently yet are a key to developing a more learning-centered environment in our schools.

Through reflection and collaborative conversation, a team or small group within the team can identify a handful of learning priorities or objectives essential to their growth and professional development. These recommendations could then be taken up in their local study teams or be the basis for training provided on an upcoming professional development day. The team could decide to devote part of meetings to new research articles regarding these objectives and make immediate progress in this area. This enables teacher leaders to control their progress and to navigate their own journey.

Virtual Learning Partners Strategy

To promote transcendent thinking, learning for teachers must be expanded beyond school walls. With advancements in technology, there is no reason why thoughtful teacher leaders, acting as Learning Advocates, can't create a virtual learning space. This way, colleagues who face similar challenges from around the world can pull together and meet regularly, to grow, evolve, and learn from one another.

Emergent teacher leaders recognize that the best ideas to transform their profession may not necessarily come from the energetic colleague down the hall. They may come from inspired colleagues in Finland, Singapore, or New Zealand. By pulling our intellectual resources together, we can become a more fluid and effective profession.

In business, the idea of partnering can create issues with proprietary challenges and market share. We are fortunate to work in a profession where everyone wins through our collaboration efforts. Thanks to technology, today's school teams actively seek out virtual partners as a mechanism for advancing their learning and stimulating growth.

To strengthen this strategy, teams should reach out to other teacher efforts in the region or around the world and remain connected to share results of their ongoing collaborations. Formally building this into the process will help everyone improve their learning.

Provide Learning Rewards Strategy

Recently, there has been a tremendous increase in the number of teachers in P–12 education pursuing master's degrees in areas related to curriculum instruction and learning outcomes (Clotfelter, Ladd, & Vigdor, 2007). This increase in classroom-based advanced degrees proves that the rigors of P–12 education have forced teachers to do exactly what we are talking about in this chapter—embrace deeper levels of learning. Teaching is becoming a highly technical field and what needs to be learned continues to evolve.

Many teachers in the past viewed "advancement" as the process of learning about school administration, then "moving up the ranks" to assistant principal, then principal. The profession has advanced from that view, however, in that growth now revolves around what teachers learn and how they put this new learning to work at key points in their career.

The best teacher leaders who advocate learning will pursue master's, doctorate, or post-bachelor's certification in areas related to the science of learning and/or some specific issue dealing with advanced pedagogy. While schools shouldn't dictate what teachers and staff choose to study at the graduate level, it doesn't hurt to mention the importance of graduate degrees related to the science of learning. Celebrating and broadcasting the efforts of teachers who pursue graduate learning in these areas will only help appreciate learning as a professional scholarly pursuit.

Graduate School Learning Cohort Strategy

One of the most empowering steps we can take as teacher leaders to make our learning experiences valuable is to pursue a post-bachelor's or master's certification, a master's degree, or a doctorate degree within some type of cohort structure. Effective teacher leaders who advocate learning pursue advanced degrees, abandon the old paradigm of working in isolation, and instead make the pursuit a collegial one.

Groups of teachers can choose team-learning projects that benefit the students they serve. Instead of developing a pseudo assignment, teachers pursuing advanced degrees together can choose a challenge in their own building. They could use the backdrop of studying for their degree as an impetus to find answers and resources to reveal better strategies or approaches.

This type of learning makes sense from a collegial standpoint. It helps build a stronger local team and allows for practical application. Thanks to the availability of distance learning, teams of teachers can study with institutions of higher education from all over the world.

Due to this competition, universities are increasingly flexible in working with teams of teachers who decide that studying together makes greater professional sense. Sometimes universities even offer individual discounts for teachers who come together in a school district or in a regional cohort and work together in their degree pursuit.

This type of collaboration is a win-win proposition for everyone involved. The universities benefit from having dedicated groups that encourage each other to finish the program, thus reducing the dropout rate. Teachers benefit because they have colleagues to support them and can reflect collaboratively with people they already know and work with. The school benefits from the learning of a group of dedicated professionals, all working together to grow in their scholarship and as professionals in the field. The momentum created by this type of collaboration provides unique opportunities.

Read, Reflect, and Report Strategy

Experiencing something new or reading unfamiliar material gives us an opportunity to compare new content against an existing body of knowledge. What learning theory has taught us is that most deep learning doesn't happen immediately. We read the information and then, after some time spent grappling with the knowledge, new levels of learning and understanding emerge (Lee & Birdsong Sabatino, 1998; Stout, 2006). The ideas that you are reading about in this book will only be valuable to you if you adopt reflection strategies that allow for enhanced learning.

The ability of a teacher leader to model reflection is driven by a multitude of factors, such as learning style and available time in the school day. Reflection can happen spontaneously or with a formalized plan. A department chair may provide opportunities for organized reflection on best-practice instructional strategies. Some principals provide such reflection time in faculty meetings. Many PLCs offer the opportunity to discuss and reflect on new learning. Asynchronous learning spaces such as blogs or even e-mail give us a chance to read, reflect, and write.

Learning opportunities must be taken seriously if learning at the deepest levels is to be achieved in schools today. By formalizing these structures, to build reading, reflection, and reporting into the calendar, the emergence of learning advocacy is more likely to occur.

Transcendent Teacher Leaders in Action: The Learning Advocate

Each of the teacher leaders featured in Chapter 1 of this book provides a great example of what it means to be a teacher leader who focuses on learning advocacy.

Kate believed that her students had the right to learn and that learning would be the key to get them out of their compromised state of illiteracy and embrace a new future. While she believed in personal responsibility and discipline, she kept their learning at the forefront of her efforts. Kate recognized that she, too, would need to keep learning as she began teaching in an unfamiliar social context in a discipline she needed to master. It was her dedication to her students' learning that drove her agenda to change her students, her school, and ultimately herself.

Khris also kept learning as the focal point of her efforts in leading the construction of a new school in Afghanistan. While these efforts certainly provided material support for a region in need, the goal of having an impact on learning was still evident—with her students as well as the Afghan students going to school for the first time.

Mary Ann understood the sacred exchange between a teacher and her students and created the best possible learning environment. She excelled as an instructor because she understood that her efforts were all about stimulating learning and adding to the knowledge of the students she served.

Finally, while many coaches lead from a deficit model, pointing out weaknesses and at times embarrassing their players in hopes of inspiring a better performance, Jim believed that the key to the greatness of his players was their ability to apply their new learning.

How would a focus on learning advocacy change the culture and climate in your school? Are there teachers in your school who are well-intentioned, but are too focused on teaching as opposed to learning? Part of the job of a fervent teacher leader is to help his or her colleagues place the emphasis where it belongs. Are you the type of teacher leader who can passionately advocate for learning in the name of driving this type of change in your school?

Conclusions

Learning advocacy is a job that is never completed. Even the most passionate Learning Advocates can become distracted by the daily grind that immerses all of us. We encourage you to begin seeing yourself as a Learning Advocate in your school. In thinking about the old images of teaching, it is likely that you will recall a focus on teaching rather than learning.

Classic depictions in the media or literature often illustrate the teaching profession as an instructor performing in front of his or her class. Making the shift from teaching to learning is one that many of us will need to be very deliberate about if we are going to make the transition necessary to lead significant levels of change. We hope that as you look into the mirror, the image of the teacher leader as Learning Advocate will become increasingly clear and help promote your leadership practice as you move ahead.

We've chosen the light bulb to be the symbol for the Learning Advocate because we believe the Learning Advocate's job is to illuminate. While teachers love the feeling of watching the light bulb flash on in a students' head, the Learning Advocate knows how to make that happen everywhere they go. They are constantly bringing new learning opportunities to light for those with whom they work. We hope that you can see yourself as the Learning Advocate, illuminating the work of others and stimulating a richer learning environment for everyone around you.

3

The Believer

Live your beliefs and you can turn the world around.
—Henry David Thoreau

The Believer Defined

The Believer is an extremely influential teacher leader whose power and influence emanates from an uncompromising reservoir of passion. Passionate teacher leaders believe in their students, colleagues, parents, and the community. They are proud to be teachers and believe in the lofty aspirations of their profession. Believers know that anything is possible. Yet, at the same time, they remain realistic. They know the pitfalls of teaching and that their professional lives will likely include many mistakes, disappointments, and mishaps. The Believer isn't defined by these moments, however. Instead, they face both victory and defeat with a deep sense of hope, courage, and patience. Unselfishly, they know that the greatness that lies ahead for the profession may emerge when their time in the classroom is done. They know that their efforts pave the way for new and better outcomes. In the end, these inspired teacher leaders know that their work in the classroom is worth fighting for and their hope is at the root of who they are. Their belief is the source of their greatness in the profession.

Why We Need the Believer

To lead transformational change in education, we need leaders who believe to their core that deep, substantive change is possible. Several years ago, a young, second-year teacher named Traci told us, "I became a teacher because I wanted to change the world. During my first year, my coteacher told me, 'Don't worry about changing the world. Just teach math!'" Unfortunately, what Traci's veteran colleague failed to recognize was that most transformational change in education and beyond emerges from simple yet profound efforts extended in small and humble ways. Traci's efforts might inspire untold levels of change in her profession and she might inspire students who go on to change the world.

While there is no end to the forces that can discourage or limit our sense of what we can become in education, in most cases, our progress is determined more by the limits of our imagination than by our professional capacities or opportunities. Teacher leaders who are Believers understand that only by breaking through these limitations can we approach the deepest levels of change. Their efforts and attitudes keep the passion for the profession and all of its possibilities alive within us. Believers replace long-held skepticism with hope and recognize that the key to reaching exalted levels in the profession is simply to believe that you can.

The Believer: Advantages and Benefits

They Create an Atmosphere That Is Both Optimistic and Realistic

A teacher leader who operates as a Believer will recognize two important things related to deep school change. First, the Believer knows that no matter how difficult their challenges may be, they know of teachers who have faced even more difficult circumstances and accomplished amazing things.

Second, Believers know that change does not happen overnight. In fact, slow and substantive change often emerges with a whisper, not a roar. But Believers know that the quiet whispers of change can build to a majestic roar of transformation.

They Create a Culture of Courageousness and Willingness to Try

Unfortunately, the image of the negative, disengaged teacher is all too common in the media, especially in literature and the movies. Most teachers enter the profession for all the right reasons and even after decades remain confident about their capacity to influence others and their deeply held beliefs and hopes for their profession.

This optimism is not often expressed, however, and may go dormant over time. Often, teachers who are outwardly negative and purposefully disengaged were once just the opposite. They only became embittered when they absorbed some hurt or frustration.

What this means for teacher leadership is that every school has untapped reservoirs of courage just waiting to emerge. The Believer is the teacher leader who reawakens the passion in others and rekindles their connections to deeply held beliefs about their profession and themselves.

Some of the most negative teachers become the most passionate advocates when change is implemented and their belief is rekindled. The Believer is the type of teacher leader who creates a culture where this is possible.

They Keep Colleagues Focused on What Is Important

A hopeful, driven, and focused teacher leader as Believer is confident that his or her school can always improve. This belief—in themselves, their colleagues, and their students—can be a spark that ignites change.

What prevents many schools from making even modest improvements is the profound lack of belief that they can make any difference. This negativity keeps the focus on the gridlock, mistakes, and shortcomings of the past. Thankfully, the Believer promotes a collegial ethic of hope and the notion that if we focus on the right actions and sensibilities, we can build momentum toward better outcomes.

They Make the Work Environment More Fun, Productive, and Satisfying

When planning a vacation, we may find ourselves enjoying the anticipation almost as much as the event itself. Our capacity to visualize fun and interesting outcomes prepares us for the actual event in a way that allows us to enjoy both.

The same is true for Believers. Their optimism and ability to visualize better processes and outcomes creates a cumulative sense of helping the organization drive forward. It also brings forth a more pleasant, engaging, and fun work environment filled with hope.

Who wouldn't want to work in a place immersed in these types of feelings?

Looking in the Mirror: Becoming the Believer

Just as we asked of you in Chapter 2, please consider your existing mental models as they relate to the teacher leader as Believer. Try to evaluate your teaching practice according to this scale quickly, without analyzing it too deeply. This will provide you with an honest look at yourself in relation to this type of teacher leadership.

Discussion of Classroom Applications

Examining these competing mental models, you see again that our perspectives on teaching are still driven by formative

Classroom Applications for the Believer

Old Reflection		*New Reflection*
In the classroom, I am seen primarily as a boss and disciplinarian.	5 4 3 2 1 0 1 2 3 4 5 ←→	In the classroom, I am seen primarily as the facilitator, leader, and guide.
In my classroom, I am the primary source of information.	5 4 3 2 1 0 1 2 3 4 5 ←→	In my classroom, I am the primary source of inspiration.
I fully expect students will behave and perform badly.	5 4 3 2 1 0 1 2 3 4 5 ←→	I fully expect students will exceed expectations.
In my class, my students see me as a gatekeeper.	5 4 3 2 1 0 1 2 3 4 5 ←→	In my class, my students see me as a gatecrasher.

assumptions that date back to the early twentieth century (Jones, 2000). Then, schools existed largely to exert authority and to deliver information.

It is not surprising that many teachers still feel the pressure to be the boss, disciplinarian, and disseminator of information. Historically, managers communicated with their charges only when their work was not up to standard. They set the parameters and expected workers to operate within those parameters (Eisner, 2002; Gray, 1993).

Today we know that students must prepare for a world that will be technologically advanced beyond our comprehension. Information will flow from everywhere and students will need to continue learning to navigate massive amounts of information, rather than feeling the pressure to retain it all in their heads.

Students certainly can, at times, disappoint. They will also exceed our expectations if we can envision that outcome. Clearly, teacher leaders who are Believers understand that you get from students and colleagues just about what you expect to get. If you expect the best, you will be rewarded.

Schoolwide Change for the Believer

Old Reflection		*New Reflection*
I plan for my future in my school based on the past.	5 4 3 2 1 0 1 2 3 4 5 ◄──►	The future in my school may look nothing like the past.
If parents, kids, administration, and the state and federal government all did the right things, we would improve.	5 4 3 2 1 0 1 2 3 4 5 ◄──►	Even in less-than-perfect conditions, we can lead significant change in schools.
We are glorified babysitters.	5 4 3 2 1 0 1 2 3 4 5 ◄──►	We are changing the world.
The system limits us.	5 4 3 2 1 0 1 2 3 4 5 ◄──►	We are limited only by our imagination.
We say, "Yeah, but . . ."	5 4 3 2 1 0 1 2 3 4 5 ◄──►	We say, "Why not?"
Pointing out excellence is bragging.	5 4 3 2 1 0 1 2 3 4 5 ◄──►	Pointing out excellence creates more of it.

Discussion of Schoolwide Change

When members of a school community come together to think about change, they tend to go in one of two directions. First are the schools that focus on the past and are wedded to their current systems and mental models. They visualize change only in terms of adjustments that can be made to those old assumptions within the current working conditions.

At the other end of the spectrum are the schools that approach change by looking forward. School leaders try to visualize a completely new approach with potentially transformative outcomes. Rather than tinkering with the details around the edges, this perspective gets at the heart of transformative influences and allows organizations to think beyond what is hindering the acceptance of new mental models. Today, Believers have enough optimism to visualize a future that might outpace anything they had hoped for in the past.

We must also keep in mind that our profession has been obsessed with the pursuit of what is average. We tend to push students to a standard, ask employees to work to rule, and measure progress by our ability to "get a C." The Believer, however, recognizes that excellence in the profession isn't achieved by aiming at the middle. Instead, there may be untold growth opportunities available if we can visualize new outcomes as a possibility.

Strategies for Becoming and Supporting the Believer

Evolving into the role of teacher leader as Believer is not about blind faith. Although these types of teacher leaders tend to have a good attitude, Believers are more than feel-good types warming up the school with daily pleasantries. Instead, these are the courageous souls who invest their hope and faith in a long-term vision of growth and improvement.

These teachers understand that better outcomes require a balance between their highest aspirations and the limits and hindrances of the moment. Believers working at the highest levels promote a climate of belief that permeates the organization.

Consider the following strategies if you are interested in becoming a Believer.

Pick Five Strategy

The Believer constantly looks for examples of ordinary schools that accomplish extraordinary things. The Believer shares these stories with friends and colleagues as examples of what schools can accomplish if they come together and focus on their goals. These models also motivate the Believer to help create a school climate where there is a greater sense that anything is possible. The Pick Five Strategy we recommend involves identifying five of these schools as models for growth and improvement and for strategic comparison.

Two of the schools chosen in the Pick Five Strategy should be ones achieving outstanding results. Ideally, these two schools will be similar in community expectations and demographics: The greater the similarity, the greater the impact on the belief system of the school making the comparison.

The next two schools picked should be similar to the Believer's current school, yet achieving slightly better results. Thus, four of the schools selected should show achievement at higher levels than the Believer's school, but at the same time providing a gradated view of good and outstanding achievement. Comparing the Believer's school to a building performing at the highest levels can be intimidating, but keeping the interim reference points in mind reinforces belief that such results can be achieved over time.

Finally, the last school identified in the Pick Five Strategy should be one that is similar to the Believer's school, but perhaps a year or two ahead in the change process. The purpose here is to establish a collegial partner in growth. The two schools can join forces to study the success patterns of the higher-performing buildings and keep each other on track in moving toward a clearer vision of what works and what doesn't work. Eventually, with more schools looking for collegial support, it's likely that other schools will identify your school someday as one to watch.

The ultimate advantage of the Pick Five Strategy is that it helps the Believer remind his or her colleagues that better performance is within reach, and that staying connected with these real-life exemplars will help. The strategy also forces schools to challenge local paradigms and limiting beliefs. When the school next door overcomes a difficult challenge with relative ease, their pathway is illuminating and can help other schools look beyond localized perceptions that may be holding them back.

Immediate Action Strategy

Many times, teacher leaders with a strong desire to make a difference become discouraged by a lack of progress. To protect against this, we recommend the Immediate Action Strategy. When an ambitious goal is set during a school improvement planning or visioning session, a team may get excited about the possibilities that lie ahead and find themselves flooded with positive feelings and emotional expectations.

Even when these good feelings abound, there can be an undercurrent of doubt as group members ask themselves whether this type of change is possible in their school. To ease the doubt, the Believer can turn to the Immediate Action Strategy and vow to recommend steps that can be taken quickly toward achievement of the new goals.

It is preferable if the group doesn't leave the meeting without knowing what actions will be taken, the dates they are to be completed, and the system that will be used for follow-up. By taking immediate action, teams see the vision they created begin to take shape and keep emotions engaged.

When someone decides to run a marathon, the dream gets very real when they turn off the alarm clock and their feet hit the street on that first day of training. They don't even have to run very far; the dream becomes more tangible with even the slightest evidence of progress. When schools get in the habit of taking small but immediate action, it instills a culture of belief and teacher leaders as Believers can more easily emerge.

Reflection, Focus, Celebrate, and Reinforce Strategy

We will address the merits of individual and team reflection throughout this book. It is a valuable tool when used to clarify goals and analyze action steps and points of progress. But reflection also helps us learn more about ourselves.

By taking time to reflect, focus, and celebrate even small increments of success, teams reinforce the notion that their actions do make a difference. Reflection on strategy and analysis of results allows teams to make changes as needed. When things go well, even in a small way, teams should reinforce their efforts with a celebration.

Emotion is still a big part of the learning process, and we tend to want to repeat those actions that make us feel good. So celebrating is a great motivator. When we celebrate even the smallest victory, we are likely to push even harder for change. This way we become a team of Believers that celebrates the rewards our belief has brought us thus far.

Lab Coat Strategy for Addressing Resistance

Unfortunately, nonbelievers can have quite a negative effect on teachers trying to become Believers. The nonbelievers try to make Believers feel foolish for striving for something more, and their negative influence may keep would-be Believers from reaching out and starting their own journeys in belief.

This is a result of both the fear of and aspirations for change are always tied closely to the emotions they create. The Lab Coat Strategy is designed to disengage the brooding emotional volley that often ensues in times of change and instead focus on the identification of real issues by seeking facts with logical pursuits.

Keep in mind, naysayers are often afraid that a potential change could make them appear less competent and will use intimidation to create a toxic emotional environment to block the change. To disengage this toxicity, the Believer can encourage a thoughtful, strategic discussion about the merits of their points in relation to current professional knowledge about the issue at hand.

The naysayer may have some valid points. Dealing with these points in a logical, scientific, lab coat–type environment makes more sense for everyone involved and will help move the school in the direction of a more sustainable change effort.

For example, if a team of Believers proposes a significant change in the organization of the school day, they may hear some negative responses from naysayers, warning of apocalyptic challenges, problems, or other detractors every time the

Believers begin to talk about the change. Approaching the problem logically, the Believer should block out a time for everyone to get together to list grievances, concerns, and fears all at one time. Then participants can reflect on those issues and discuss how they impact the change process. By taking time to examine these negatives, even opponents may be willing to engage in an organized brainstorming session wherein all the potential benefits could be explored as well.

Taking time to explore these issues comprehensively while allowing those negative aspects of change to be presented and fully explored provides a cathartic opportunity for everyone. Thoughtfully reflecting in a scientific manner, rather than in an accusatory way, allows others to have their concerns addressed, and the team may discover they no longer need to be intimidated by those who feared the change process. It's a valuable lesson for the team to face a challenge, and turn out to be wise and talented enough to overcome it.

Change Warrior Strategy

Believers will encounter many challenges while attempting to lead significant change in their school. Saboteurs are always lurking and can present a significant hindrance to change efforts.

Saboteurs are more dangerous than naysayers in that they are not just afraid of change and potential failures; they take direct overt or covert action in an attempt to derail any change effort that they don't agree with. The Believer has to be courageous and directly confront these behaviors to ensure that there is collegial support. This creates an environment that does not allow the saboteur to continue.

Confronting saboteurs takes courage. We encourage teacher leaders to adopt a change warrior mentality and be brave enough to confront this behavior in a fair, direct manner. If saboteurs choose to attack Believers and other types of teacher leaders in public, it is important to respond to these attacks in the moment. A bullying atmosphere can have an extremely negative effect on school culture and it is difficult to believe if no one is courageous enough to stand up to the resistors, especially if those attacks are malicious.

We are not advocating civil war, but we believe many change efforts in schools are derailed when a larger crowd of well-intended teachers are unwilling to stand up to a small, but emotionally bound group of determined saboteurs. Some change is worth defending and teacher leaders who are Believers will be change warriors who confront saboteurs when necessary.

Over the years, saboteurs have derailed significant levels of change, and well-intending teachers have at times shrugged their shoulders and waited for the principal to stop this onslaught of negativity. While the best schools have principals who are willing to confront saboteurs, we are in an age of reform today where the highly technical nature of the profession, the sheer number of teachers, and the complexity of our systems of communication have created an environment where we simply cannot wait for the best and bravest principals to confront those teachers who seek to derail change. As teacher leaders, we have to be willing to take them on ourselves.

Articulated Beliefs Strategy

Finally, one of the most powerful strategies Believers can use is to articulate a set of beliefs that accurately represent their views on students, school, their profession, their colleagues, and their mission in their work. Such articulated beliefs enable Believers to know themselves better and be able to take more direct action in pursuit of their objectives. Below are examples of belief statements that the authors have written to help you think about your beliefs.

1. I believe our profession can change the world.
2. I believe the change we lead will be difficult and I expect to be challenged in every way.

3. I believe the colleagues I work with are an invaluable resource to me and I hope I can be a support to them.
4. I believe that change in school is possible when I learn something new and apply that new learning in class with my students.
5. I believe the things I do today in my class could resonate with my students for a lifetime.
6. I believe by working together as a team, we can fundamentally change the school for the better.
7. I believe there will always be challenges and those challenges will serve to make us wiser and even more prepared to lead the changes that matter.

Transcendent Teacher Leaders in Action: The Believer

The story of Kate at the beginning of the book demonstrates what is possible when teacher leaders believe in their students, their profession, and themselves. As former English and reading teachers, it is hard for us to fathom the leaps Kate's students achieved in their reading levels. Even in the face of doubting experts and critical colleagues, Kate was driven to greatness as a teacher leader by having the unique capacity to conjure up enough belief to make the transformation possible.

Many of Mary Ann's colleagues questioned how cooperative learning would work in a tough, urban classroom. They doubted that she could apply the model with any consistency and they certainly did not believe that she would meet her goal of using the model every day, improving the culture and climate of her classroom, and enhancing student performance. But she did. It was Mary Ann's belief in her own professional capacity to learn, grow, and evolve, as well as her belief in the students she served, that made all the difference in powering her transformation.

Khris's journey would appear to be the most perilous and difficult to believe. It must have been very lonely at times when resistors emerged and her goal felt out of reach. Her unique ability as a Believer allowed her to not only lead, but to engender that sense of belief in others. This was the difference that allowed Khris and her students to forever change a small corner of the world.

For Jim, there were a number of people who were surprised when his football team became competitive at the local level. And no one but Jim thought the team could be a state contender. Like Khris, Jim had the unique capacity to capture his belief, share it with others, and get fellow teachers, coaches, parents, and players to adopt the belief and embrace the possibility ahead.

Can you imagine what your school would be like if you had one or two more teacher leaders who truly exemplified what it means to be the Believer? Even one motivated teacher leader who grasps the concept of belief could truly transform the classroom, the school, and the community by igniting passion and following his or her dreams. It would be easy to say that the teacher leader as Believer sounds like hyperbole. But the stories presented here are real and there are undoubtedly teachers out there today on similar missions. Their belief is the power behind the transformations they are leading. Are you a teacher leader who has this capacity? How could you change your world with the infusion of belief?

Conclusions

The teacher leader as Believer can have a profound impact on a school. When thinking about images of teaching, the concept of Believer may not be as foreign to you as some of the others presented in this book. You might have imagined yourself as the teacher who would be there for your students, believing in them and supporting their growth along the way. Any experienced teacher knows, however, that it is easy to get distracted from this notion of belief as a mechanism for leading change.

We encourage you to redouble your efforts in this area. Think about your own image of teaching. How could applying what it means to be the Believer reshape your practice and potentially drive significant levels of change in your school? Do you believe?

B The Believer

The symbol we've chosen for the Believer is a heart because the Believer engages our learning and growth by connecting to the heart. These special teacher leaders have bigger hearts than most and this symbol helps illustrate that fact. We hope that in visualizing this symbol and thinking about your role as the Believer, you can be that teacher with a giant heart who helps those hearts around you grow as well.

4

The Transformationalist

Vision is the art of seeing the invisible.

—Jonathon Swift

The Transformationalist Defined

The Transformationalist is a teacher leader with an acute capacity to visualize, articulate, and then implement an ambitious, inspiring, and transformative vision for change. These teacher leaders can visualize an outlandishly successful outcome with great levels of Monday-morning specificity and readiness. They are willing to lead and follow in numerous ways en route to these loftier destinations. Transformationalists have the capacity to see things the way they are and then visualize with clarity better outcomes on the horizon and the pathway they must take to get there.

Why We Need the Transformationalist

Truly transformative change is difficult. Well-intentioned traditional leaders whose work is in an office and not the classroom may speak of transformative change in their school; however, most often their perspective leaves them unable to conceptualize the moment-by-moment execution of that transformation with students in the classroom. Since deep change in schools must be defined by what happens in the classroom between students and teachers, it's clear that the teachers themselves must lead this change.

In an era in which the profession continues to struggle with finding principals and other school leaders with knowledge and experience, teacher leaders who operate as Transformationalists will be key to improving schools in the future. Thus, we need to develop transformational leadership capacity in teachers with a clear vision of how change in the classroom occurs and the steps we must take to get there.

THE TRANSFORMATIONALIST: ADVANTAGES AND BENEFITS

They Are Willing to Redefine the Profession, Their Work, and Themselves

Most of us are nervous about change. Even if we support the notion that growth is a positive thing, actually changing how we work and approach our daily challenges tends to inspire, even in the best of us, a degree of fear. The Transformationalist, however, acknowledges this emotional tendency, can visualize the steps needed to make dramatic changes, and works each day to achieve these goals.

The Transformationalist is willing to rethink major assumptions within the profession and bring an entrepreneurial spirit to the process. These leaders have an uncompromising capacity to bravely reconsider essential aspects of what they do in the name of determining the best models for change.

They Move Quickly From Conversation to Planning for Action

Anyone reading this book can identify with those optimistic moments when educators get together and dream about transcendent goals. Emotions run high as they talk about what great results they could achieve if only such change were to occur. These moments of inspiration often don't last, and we return to our old habits.

The Transformationalist is good at keeping these magic moments from slipping away by quickly getting specific and strategic about what is needed to implement the change. Instead of just watching great ideas fade away, the Transformationalist inspires others to take ideas to the next level.

Constructing such a vision is a complex mental process that involves a number of steps. Our brains have to navigate a series of complex gyrations to create a unique mental representation or vision (Reason, 2010). The Transformationalist has the mental ability to do the hard work of taking the hopes and aspirations of others and turning them into reality.

They Own the Process

Ultimately, the Tranformationalist helps create a school culture where teachers can take a greater degree of ownership of the change process. This, in itself, is likely to inspire a greater degree of collegial commitment to the transformation efforts.

Looking in the Mirror: Becoming the Transformationalist

Once again, consider your existing mental models as they relate to the teacher leader as Transformationalist. Try to quickly evaluate your teaching practice according to this scale. This will provide you an honest look at yourself in relation to this type of teacher leadership.

Discussion of Classroom Applications

Teacher leaders invested in the art of transformation aren't willing to live with old definitions of what it means to teach. Like most professions, changes in cultural

Classroom Applications for the Transformationalist

Old Reflection		*New Reflection*
Others have defined teaching; I am living their definition.	54321012345 ◄——►	I am redefining teaching every day in my classroom.
Others have defined what I teach.	54321012345 ◄——►	What I teach is constantly being transformed by changes in the world around us. Therefore, my approaches must always be transforming as well.
I make subtle changes to my performance throughout my career in hopes of continuous improvement.	54321012345 ◄——►	I am willing to completely transform my work as a teacher in the name of improving service and keeping up with changes in the culture.

expectations and possibility redefine every aspect of our work. Transformationalists fully expect that as long as they teach, their approach to the profession will have to continue to evolve. As a result, you may see Transformationalists take chances in the classroom with strategies, approaches, and activities that might be considered novel.

For these teachers, looking into that mirror isn't easy and even well-intentioned, optimistic, hard-working professionals can't always see their own gifts. While there are teacher leaders who can be optimistic, helpful, and determined, teacher leaders who are Transformationalists, who can visualize and implement innovative classroom applications, truly meet the definition of unique.

Schoolwide Change for the Transformationalist

Old Reflection		*New Reflection*
Dreams of change are nice, but most of the time we just talk and nothing happens.	5 4 3 2 1 0 1 2 3 4 5 ←→	Dreams of change are nice, but I know how to change those dreams into a vision and a plan.
A comprehensive school-reform plan will be difficult to implement. I hope administration will remember the details.	5 4 3 2 1 0 1 2 3 4 5 ←→	A comprehensive school-reform plan will be difficult to implement. I hope that we can work together and establish a strategy that works for everyone.
Our principal doesn't know who the key decision makers are in this building. Without their approval, this change process will fail. I hope he does something about it soon.	5 4 3 2 1 0 1 2 3 4 5 ←→	Our principal doesn't understand who the key decision makers are in this building. Without their approval, this change process will fail. We should go to those decision makers and see if we can identify issues and opportunities.

Discussion of Schoolwide Change

Viewing the old leadership paradigms compared to what it means to be a Transformationalist, we see the importance of belief and ownership. Transformationalists do not view improved outcomes as a well-intentioned abstraction. Instead, they have a clear idea of what could happen. They can also identify the steps it will take to arrive at that outcome.

This capacity to visualize a specific outcome and identify a path toward it requires focus and maturity in a teacher leader.

Transformationalists are unique in their ability to construct a vision, and causing the rest of us to be moved, engaged, and motivated by their efforts.

Strategies for Becoming and Supporting the Transformationalist

Teacher leaders who evolve into Transformationalists bear substantial influence over others and can have a profound impact on change. The development of a transformative school culture led by thoughtful teacher leaders, however, is a process that takes time. Below are strategies formulated to stimulate transformational perspectives and encourage new Transformationalists to emerge.

Leadership and Power Orientation Strategy

The best schools today don't necessarily associate leadership with a particular person or position. Principals, assistant principals, curriculum directors, and department chairs may represent the leadership and power structure in the school as defined by some organizational chart. The best schools today, however, aren't limited by these hierarchies on paper and see leadership as a force that emerges from any level of the organization (Reason, 2010).

In every school we have worked with, there is generalized agreement that some of the most powerful leaders in the school don't necessarily have titles. They are the ones who ultimately dictate whether a change is successful or not and everyone else involved knows it.

One of the most powerful steps a school can take to enact transformative change is to have direct, focused conversations about leadership, power, and those factors that influence change in your school. For example, if a school is struggling with its math scores, a team may be formed to address the issue. Team members may acknowledge that technology, textbooks, and curriculum decisions lie primarily with the central office. They may also recognize that the principal and building-level administration control schedules and local intervention efforts. So, what other power sources exist? What power does the staff have in influencing these scores?

In the course of this conversation, team members may realize that they have the most influence in this process. They control how they approach the students each day and the strategies associated with instruction.

Thus, the value of the Leadership and Power Orientation Strategy is that it allows teams of teachers and administrators to be realistic about their capacities to influence change. If district-level funding isn't available for technology and material choices, what leadership can be exerted at the building level to get what's needed? If building administration isn't able to support change, what steps can the teachers themselves take to achieve the transformation they seek? By being clear about the genesis of change and the opportunities available, teams can realistically expect teacher leaders at all levels to influence potential solutions.

When executing this strategy, it's helpful to make it a part of a meeting agenda. The process of visualizing change should include a discussion of leadership and power. If the meeting includes leaders from the central office, the building, and the classroom, each group can influence any transformative proposal. If the meeting consists only of teachers, it's best to limit the conversation to those changes that the teachers have the power to initiate.

Lab Coat Transformation Plan Strategy

The lab coat analogy is used to encourage teachers to see themselves as tactical scientists approaching an emotionally bound change. When facing a significant transformational change, emotions are likely to run high as numerous individuals are suddenly asked to push themselves to new levels of performance far outside their comfort zone.

Conducting a lab coat discussion in this context means that teacher leaders should hold an honest conversation with as little emotion as possible regarding the potentially upsetting aspects of the change process. We encourage teacher leaders to put on their white lab coats and think deeply about how those around them will be affected by the change they are recommending. We urge them to identify what might be emotional concerns.

With a directed emotional focus, individuals and groups become more neurologically engaged and can learn and do more (Chen, Tjosvold, & Liu, 2006). These lab coat discussions are strategic in that they help the teacher leader as Transformationalist anticipate and prepare for the reactions that lie ahead, and can lead to more successful outcomes.

Vision Construction Strategy

We have made the case that the Transformationalist has to develop a capacity to present a clear and inspiring vision for change, then work to articulate the steps that can be taken to shape that vision. The visualization and construction processes are rarely done well alone and in many cases the Transformationalist's greatest strength is supporting the team while building this vision and identifying the processes.

The Transformationalist understands that the mental process of constructing a collective vision is a challenging one and the ability to construct these mental representations is driven by our individual and collective history, our shared mental models, and our expectations or learning context (Braine, 2009). The neurological process of constructing an individual and collective mental representation is very complex. Thus, we recommend that Transformationalists keep a couple of simple things in mind. First, dialogue and collaboration are extremely important and second, the more significant the change, the more time for reflection and discussion is needed.

What the Transformationalist can do during these reflection opportunities is to listen carefully to the discussions emerging within the group, then encourage each group member to dig deeper in their exploration of how they visualize the change and the challenges ahead. These discussions will reveal different mental models regarding the change and differences related to experience and context that might drive various perspectives and aspirations. Digital natives and digital immigrants, for example, might view some changes as more or less intrusive to their teaching habits based on their history and how they learn today. In the final analysis, the Transformationalist can encourage the deepest change in their school by helping the teams they work with continuously clarify their vision for change and how that change is implemented.

We recommend that teams come together whenever possible and review their vision for change. Periodically letting everybody take a turn to describe his or her mental image of the change will help identify what might be disconnects in the process. This may actually help to engineer a much-needed tune-up in the direction of the change. At our best, we are moving in pursuit of a vision. Transformational teacher leaders consistently revisit and reconstruct that vision so we know where we're going.

People-Centered Change Strategy

When it comes to change, we tend to focus on aspects such as new schedules, curriculum, or course materials. The teacher leader who operates as a Transformationalist believes that any successful evolution starts first with people.

In applying the People-Centered Change Strategy, teams develop awareness of their focus when talking about change. For example, a building may adopt a new reading curriculum in an attempt to improve elementary student literacy. It's tempting when discussing this change to talk about the new materials and implementations the teachers will soon share. These are ancillary, however, to the real changes going on.

The real changes involve teachers learning new strategies to help students improve their reading. The curriculum and other supports are there to help teachers and students work together better. It may seem like only a subtle difference, but focusing on change as it relates to "people," as opposed to a new textbook, affects how schools think about improvement and may directly impact how they approach the change process itself.

Inaction Visualization Strategy

Transformation is driven by action. A clear vision gives direction and actions make movement toward that outcome a reality. The establishment of a vision and the execution of action steps build momentum toward meaningful transformation.

One way to motivate transformation is to consider the implications of inaction. We recommend that teams immersed in the change process build in opportunities to reflect on the costs and implications of inaction. What will happen in the organization if, instead of working toward this new vision and taking dramatic action, we do nothing? What is the cost of inaction to students and the community?

Holding an honest conversation about what may happen if you don't move forward can inspire teams to overcome their fears. Inaction can derail momentum, deprive students of an opportunity to learn skills they need to be successful, and have real social and economic impacts. Taking action requires courage and the teacher leader as Transformationalist can inspire courage by helping his or her team understand what will happen if they do nothing.

Reflect on Process and Progress of Transformation Strategy

Have you ever felt discouraged and then reflected on how far you've come, realizing that you're actually doing better than you thought? Maybe one day you began to criticize yourself about something, only to realize that you were doing well in a number of other areas and, upon reflection, began to feel better about yourself? This is a natural tendency that we all exhibit from time to time. What this type of thinking shows us is the value of reflection.

Reflection helps us realize the strengths and limitations of our efforts to improve. We recommend that teacher leaders who are serious about becoming Transformationalists strategically build in time for reflection. This way, teams can have an honest discussion about the progress they're making toward substantive change.

For example, when a team makes a significant change in an academic area, members may feel overwhelmed thinking about the big-picture changes ahead. Remember, progress and momentum can be bolstered by taking immediate action toward a change. Reflection can play a similar role. By stopping to reflect on all of the good things that have happened and all of the progress that's been made, the team may feel a renewed commitment to the change effort. We may be momentarily discouraged by what seems like a long journey. But by stopping to look back, teams may recognize the progress and be inspired to press on.

These strategic planning moments don't have to be protracted opportunities to pat ourselves on the back. During these moments of reflection, we may decide that we aren't making enough progress and need to redouble our efforts. By stopping to reflect, everyone in the group has the chance to be held accountable and recalibrate their efforts in moving toward a profound transformation. This is a small step that makes transformational change much more likely to occur.

Transcendent Teacher Leaders in Action: The Transformationalist

Each of the teacher leaders featured in Chapter 1 led a change that was truly transformational. While other passionate educators may have a sensibility that things could be better, the Transformationalist is a teacher leader with a very specific and acute vision for change that represents a dramatic departure from the past.

Mary Ann's transformation from traditional teacher to one who achieved outstanding results came thanks to her adoption of cooperative learning strategies, which required her to have a vision for a different type of classroom.

Kate didn't just seek to help her ninth graders pass their core subjects their freshman year. Instead, she transformed the expectation to not only graduating, but going on to college as well. With a population of students who viewed graduation as improbable, Kate visualized the specific strategies required to get them past graduation and on to higher education, demonstrating her capacity to visualize a different outcome and execute the plan to near perfection.

Similarly, Khris took a teachable moment and offered a life-changing chance to serve others. While many of us have benevolent intentions and may do what we can to help our fellow man, Khris had a unique vision for what was possible. She was able to think systematically, executing each step, and leading an extraordinary change in one small corner of the world.

Jim also had to facilitate a complete transformation of his school's football program. It involved a transformation of the expectations of students, coaches, and parents. It required a transformation in practice habits and off-season conditioning. There was even a transformation in what it meant to field a team and the steps the school would take to reach out to students and keep them involved with the team. While most coaches have the desire to win, having the transformative vision and the ability to execute it is a special talent in teacher leadership.

You may be a trifle intimidated after reading each of these individual's stories and wonder if you are a teacher leader who can facilitate transformational change. While it is true that certain teacher leaders are better at visualizing a specific outcome than others, we must keep in mind that transformations can be large and small. Mary Ann's transformation didn't set the world on fire, but it led to significant changes for the students involved.

As teacher leaders, we hope you give thought to what your school would be like if you sought to not only make changes around the edges, but to truly transform your professional practice at the heart. What if there were several teacher leaders in your building who could articulate a transformational vision and had the energy and dedication to follow through? Would that make a difference to the level of engagement in your school? Would it add interest and excitement to your time together at work? Can you emerge as a teacher leader as Transformationalist?

Conclusions

Unfortunately, the prevailing image of teaching revolves almost exclusively around the teachers' work in the classroom with the students they serve. Each of the examples of teacher leaders in Chapter 1 embodies what it means to be transformational. Many of their actions in achieving those transformations, however, took place outside the classroom and involved a significant emotional shift in pursuit of the outcomes they were after. Put simply, their transformation involved multiple facets of their personal and professional lives and involved them changing as people and learning new things about themselves while leading these important journeys in change.

As a new teacher, you may look in the mirror and see a teacher who is making a difference. It usually takes some time in the job, however, to truly comprehend the type of transformation that's possible when we pull together and dedicate ourselves to change. Conversely, the hypnosis of our day-to-day activities can diminish our vision and put us on a pathway toward outcomes that are far too pedestrian. You didn't become a teacher to simply get a few more students to state standard next year. You didn't become a teacher to help facilitate modest improvements in the lives of your students. These aren't the challenges that stir our blood. We hope you are the type of teacher leader who can inspire yourself and others to become truly transformational in both your capacity to envision better outcomes and to take the actions to make your dreams come true. Are you a transformational teacher leader?

The symbol of the Transformationalist is the rising star because this teacher leader helps those around him or her reach exalted levels by encouraging them to shoot for higher ground than they thought was possible. We hope that in visualizing that rising star, you can see your own career emerging in ways no one could have imagined. Likewise, we hope that your efforts as a teacher leader serve to support others as their star also rises in the sky.

5

The Synergizer

Coming together is a beginning. Keeping together is progress. Working together is success.

—Henry Ford

The Synergizer Defined

Synergizers are teacher leaders who can mold a group into a team. They don't have to dominate or even "lead" in the traditional sense. They can be the glue that holds the team together. They can be the spark that ignites and inspires. They know how people work and can rewire the group to surge with newfound energy, potential, and passion. The Synergizer's unique gifts revolve around the ability to develop and nurture professional networks of support. This type of teacher leader knows where to search for answers and is willing to call upon friends or colleagues from a variety of settings to help when needed. While there is usually strength in numbers, the Synergizer knows there is even greater strength when those numbers pull together and become teams of highly effective, collegial partners who bring unprecedented power and opportunity in pursuit of any goal.

Why We Need the Synergizer

All schools today must learn that the pathway to innovation requires pooling our collective energies in a way that yields better outcomes. Bringing synergy to teams increases levels of engagement, improves focus, and helps drive improved outcomes (Achterman & Loertscher, 2008; Chapman et al., 2005). Synergizers meet people, make friends, and develop new collegial contacts for future reference. They are available to others and are ready to offer support in any way. Synergizers build new networks to call upon whenever needed to supply energy, expertise, and a fresh approach.

School challenges are rigorous and demanding. One person's resolution to a difficult challenge can give another person a new tool for moving forward. It's possible that colleagues we have not met have already faced many of our most difficult challenges. The teacher leader as Synergizer is there to make the connection.

The Synergizer: Advantages and Benefits

They Provide a Much-Needed Network of Support

The teacher leader as Synergizer never walks alone. When you ask synergistic teacher leaders for help, they immediately reflect upon their own experiences and consider knowledgeable friends and colleagues who may have insight on the challenge at hand.

Say a school faces a difficult challenge related to students transitioning from one grade to the next. Once Synergizers realize the challenge, they begin to visualize friends and colleagues with similar experiences who may be able to provide assistance. These colleagues may help to identify opportunities and consequences associated with different approaches.

The Synergizer's capacity to connect with others makes any school more flexible and effective in dealing with difficult challenges. When you make a connection with a Synergizer, you develop a collegial partner for life who will ask you to share your energy and expertise and will be there for you to return the favor.

They Skillfully Facilitate Debate and Reflection

The teacher leader as Synergizer can reach out to his or her network and gather a lengthy list of pros and cons regarding change efforts. If a community is dealing with a significant school challenge and debating potential solutions, synergistic teacher leaders can recover feedback on how the discussions or debates were conducted in their colleagues' school districts. Synergizers may request a synopsis of these discussions or may pursue primary artifacts that might help their team consider the options. They may ask to see the actual policy adopted or the contract language pursued when facing a particularly transformative change in school schedule or in the working conditions of the teacher. The Synergizer's collection of data greatly enhances the debate on change issues because fellow teachers can reflect upon a set of collegial experiences.

Highly effective teams spend a great deal of time reflecting. Thoughtful, strategic thinking is key to improving team learning (Cohen & Robertson, 2007). When facilitated appropriately, virtual or face-to-face teams can get comfortable working together and establish an improved capacity to strategically and thoughtfully reflect on possible outcomes (Merrill & Gilbert, 2008). This reflection opens the door to deeper organizational learning.

They Can Strategically Float a Trial Balloon and Test Community Support

Synergizers build a network of colleagues from diverse backgrounds and establish and maintain powerful local networks of parents and community members. These connections pay dividends at the classroom and building levels.

For one thing, local networks allow a teacher leader to launch a trial balloon to gauge community reactions to a proposed schedule change. In this way, the Synergizer can get a clear idea of how parents might feel about the proposed change. This is a valuable perspective.

Synergizers understand that *who you know* is important; staying connected with others keeps those lines of communication open.

LOOKING IN THE MIRROR: BECOMING THE SYNERGIZER

This section invites you to consider your existing mental models as they relate to those of the teacher leader as Synergizer. Try to quickly evaluate your teaching practice according to this scale. This will provide you with an honest look at yourself in relation to this type of teacher leadership.

Classroom Applications for the Synergizer

Old Reflection		*New Reflection*
I work primarily alone.	5 4 3 2 1 0 1 2 3 4 5 ⟷	I consistently work with a team.
I get ideas for teaching from the teachers I get to know.	5 4 3 2 1 0 1 2 3 4 5 ⟷	I get ideas for teaching from network spaces all over the world.
Classroom best practice is determined by local experiences and expectations.	5 4 3 2 1 0 1 2 3 4 5 ⟷	Classroom best practice is determined by national and international standards and is consistently reevaluated by teachers all over the world every day.

Discussion of Classroom Applications

Schools from the early- to mid-twentieth century were designed specifically to reduce opportunities for teachers to communicate and collaborate (Jones, 2000). The idea of teachers working together, collaborating, and creating deep levels of synergy is an idea in direct opposition to what school administrators envisioned just a few years ago.

While in recent years we have broken many barriers to collaboration, the practice of education remains one where teachers work, to a great extent, alone. The evolution of professional learning communities has helped correct this practice through increased levels of participation by teacher leaders in network spaces, in their region, and throughout the world (DuFour et al., 2008).

Connecting with others and raising the bar accomplishes for teachers what open sourcing did for software development. When new software tools are developed, they are

Schoolwide Change for the Synergizer

Old Reflection		*New Reflection*
Feedback on my teaching primarily comes from my principal.	5 4 3 2 1 0 1 2 3 4 5 ←→	Feedback on my teaching primarily comes from my network of teaching colleagues.
I wait and see what I am going to be provided in my classroom to teach.	5 4 3 2 1 0 1 2 3 4 5 ←→	My colleagues and I investigate what we need and collectively advocate for these resources.
I am very selective; I only collaborate with colleagues I have known for a while, and trust and respect.	5 4 3 2 1 0 1 2 3 4 5 ←→	I am very open; I consistently get ideas from blogs and other virtual spaces from teachers who I have never met.

shared with the outside world via the Internet. These tools are viewed and shared by others and are collectively vetted by outsiders, and in many cases altered and improved on to lead to a better design.

Teaching is a profession in which we can join together to break down the hindrances to synergy. The habits of joining together and sharing insights to improve on each other's work can lead to the kinds of innovation in the classroom that have revolutionized the world in terms of software.

Discussion of Schoolwide Change

The teaching profession continues to become increasingly technical and specialized. The ability of a principal to provide needed strategic input on the instructional process will continue to be challenged. There is just too much information for one person to consistently manage and comprehend.

Developing true synergy will allow the teaching profession to grow, evolve, and innovate, thanks to thoughtful reflection, connection, and the ability to find precise levels of input from sources well beyond the school. This will affect change. Synergistic teachers will develop the local energy to make a difference by tapping the best ideas from innumerous connections both inside and outside the profession.

Strategies for Becoming and Supporting the Synergizer

Promoting teacher leaders as Synergizers is extremely important. As you read this chapter, you may visualize teachers who behave this way or you may have adopted many of these behaviors yourself. It will take years to fully develop this essential component of teacher leadership. Schools should adopt specific actionable strategies, such as those listed below, to encourage this process.

Teacher Leadership Network Strategy

The paradigm has shifted regarding building a network. When phones were attached to the wall and letters were stamped and mailed, long-distance collaborations were difficult. Today, teachers can attend conferences and meet new colleagues they admire, and, thanks to technology, remain connected to them and continue to share ideas and resources for decades to come.

Even though networking is not a new idea and technology has been around long enough for us to appreciate its advantages, we believe that to enhance synergistic teacher leadership and to encourage significant change, a more formalized network-development process is needed. Put simply, we need to get more strategic about developing and maintaining high-functioning, flexible networks.

Teacher leaders reading this book can start by examining their own professional network. We recommend periodically going through your professional contacts and making sure that contact information is up-to-date and clear. When new contacts are made, add them to the network and include in your notes information about their specific areas of expertise.

Plan to reach out to these colleagues at least once or twice a year and update them about what you are doing in your school. This habit will become a valuable network resource for them and the power of synergy will remain engaged. When you reach out to these colleagues, you will be amazed at the feedback you receive. The tools of the profession are constantly evolving and we can only help one another if we reach out on a consistent basis. Build into your calendar opportunities to revisit your network and don't miss your deadlines!

Teams can practice developing and nurturing networks of support. Any team or group that meets consistently can put network support on the agenda. Each member can consider connections they have developed over the years and whether there is any expertise available to support the work of the team.

School improvement teams can infuse this agenda item during their time working together. Departmental or grade-level meetings can schedule network development as an agenda item at points throughout the year. Staff meetings and professional learning community collaboration time can also represent growth opportunities in developing additional formalized, strategic, and synergistic networks of support.

The idea of networking is certainly hard to challenge. Scheduling it into your individual or team work plan can bring this synergy to life, stimulating unique innovations.

National Sister School Adoption Strategy

Teacher leaders attending professional conferences often meet colleagues from schools very similar to their own. While there's nothing wrong with adding one or two teachers to your network, you can make such contacts even more powerful. When another school with similar demographics, goals, and objectives is identified, Synergizers can lead the effort to adopt that school as a state or national sister school.

Such an action allows teams of synergistic leaders to engage and resolve issues with greater levels of collaboration. Both schools can help each other challenge existing paradigms and rethink long-held beliefs or assumptions about their work and themselves. A synergistic partner pushes us to be more creative and encourages our best efforts during the collaboration process. This leads to greater accountability and competition as teams from each school compare notes on their progress.

Many schools dabble in the notion of having a collegial partner. We recommend formalizing the connection to make synergy more viable for everyone involved.

International Sister School Adoption Strategy

While similar to that of a state or national school partner, developing an international sister school has unique advantages. An international perspective brings greater diversity and new insights into problems or challenges a school encounters. Perhaps there are conventions or restrictions in U.S. schools that educators abroad simply do not face. Developing diverse learning partners in your network of like-minded Synergizers broadens perspectives and stimulates new levels of creativity.

Required Networking Construction Strategy

Many times when school personnel attend a conference, there is little expectation of tangible benefits to justify the district's investment. These days, schools ask conference attendees to bring back impressions from the conference to share with colleagues so that all can benefit.

Sharing new knowledge makes sense from a synergistic perspective. We recommend this strategy because it allows us to actively acquire new knowledge and share it with our colleagues. This process also makes us better teachers and learners. It helps to require conference attendees to bring back a bolstered network. Formalizing the expectation encourages all school personnel to return with new local, state, or national contacts that enhance networking and increase synergy.

New Teacher Wire-In Strategy

One of the most debilitating beliefs in schools is that teachers cannot lead a team until they are tenured, serve as a department chair, or teach a certain number of years to earn the right to offer an opinion. Other industries regard new employees as invaluable resources uniquely in touch with recent learning. Progressive systems feature managers who immediately infuse new employees into the system to energize the network.

We recommend that schools follow this practice. By wiring new teachers into the system immediately, they can be asked to contribute at the highest levels. Including new teachers in the fold often and early energizes the system. It can also motivate the new employees to plant their roots in the school and more immediately call it home.

Virtual Collaboration and Network Spaces Strategy

Today, there are a number of blog spaces that allow teachers to connect in new ways. Teacher leaders can build a blog of their own by using one of the vast numbers of free host spaces available (i.e., blogger.com, tumblr.com, wordpress.com, etc.). This space gives teachers a place to collaborate and explore ideas and perspectives.

We recommend that this strategy be formalized and that teams identify network spaces to use and remain dedicated to visiting and contributing to on an ongoing basis. Scheduling these activities makes it more likely they will occur and building this initiative into the agenda ensures that at least some members of the team take advantage of these collaborative spaces.

Synergy Networking and Change Strategy

Obviously, one of the quickest ways to create an environment where synergy exists is to make it mandatory. This is especially important whenever a team or school is facing significant change. For example, if the school wants to adopt a new schedule or align curriculum differently in hopes of changing instructional patterns, they will make better decisions if the team seeks a diverse set of opinions in their network. This can give the team much-needed perspective.

Anyone reading this book can certainly identify with the idea of being too close to a change effort. Receiving outside feedback enlightens the team and introduces ideas about how to improve their efforts. By making this an expectation, the organization guarantees that networking and synergy will become an integral part of the learning system and ultimately improve the school.

Transcendent Teacher Leaders in Action: The Synergizer

The transcendent teacher leaders illustrated in Chapter 1 used a great deal of synergy while leading significant levels of change.

Khris collaborated with educators, leaders, and generous benefactors from around the world on her mission to support the families in Afghanistan.

Kate's energy and enthusiasm spread throughout her school as she energized a dedicated group of teachers to join her network of passionate support. These teachers brought valuable insights with them.

Mary Ann's outstanding performance as an instructor allowed her to connect with hundreds of other teachers who adopted her strategies and approaches. Sharing her expertise, Mary Ann helped build a collegial network of teaching excellence. New levels of insight and understanding were emerging all the time.

Finally, Jim created an almost palpable level of passionate synergy with his team, their families, and those close to the program. He raised expectations and convinced those around him that his vision was achievable. Had any of these leaders worked alone, they wouldn't have gotten very far.

How might your mission be impacted if you were to embrace the tenets of the Synergizer? Are there connections out there for you to tap to improve service and support? What achievements could you lead if you developed a passionate and synergistic team that shared your goals and aspirations?

Conclusions

The goal of the Synergizer is to become an exemplary collaborator who constantly builds new connections and forever nurtures his or her current network. Synergizers seek new and improved ways to influence innovation and to connect with those who can help them change. Considering the sheer number of teachers and the technological power that holds us together, we have the ability to create synergy at unprecedented levels. Synergy gives us tools and connections that can help resolve some of our most difficult learning challenges.

Software development, the music industry, publishing, and many other professions were transformed almost overnight by the ability to connect and create new, more powerful alliances. We are all on the same team in teaching and the Synergizer can be the teacher leader who wires these networks to lead significant school change.

The image of the teacher leader as Synergizer was probably not in the mirror on your first day of school. This means that as a contemporary teacher leader, you have to set the bar for what it means to promote synergy and transform your practice with connection and collaboration. When you look in the mirror, do you see the Synergizer waiting to emerge?

For the Synergizer, we chose a symbol that we hope demonstrates motion and connectivity. The Synergizer is a teacher leader who can get us moving and takes advantage of the physics of motion, to create new and untapped sources of power and influence. The Synergizer understands how one source of power depends upon another and gains momentum by making the connections that matter. We hope you can see yourself as one of the arrows in this symbol and visualize the networks you work with as its counterpoint, connecting with one another and building momentum, power, and influence.

6

The Method Master

Without craftsmanship, inspiration is a mere reed shaken in the wind.

—Johannes Brahms

THE METHOD MASTER DEFINED

Learning is the ultimate goal for any teacher leader. The Method Master is exceptional in the art and science of selecting, learning, and applying research-based, best-practice instructional methods. The trade of these teachers is to enhance old tools and collect new ones to stimulate authentic student learning. Just like a carpenter or master craftsman, the Method Master seeks to enhance old tools and is constantly collecting new ones in hopes of stimulating authentic learning. Teacher leaders who are Method Masters come to know their tools well and use them with uncanny precision. The Method Master makes the application of high-level instructional methods look easy. The Method Master is willing to share his or her knowledge to improve the profession by helping others enhance their professional practice.

Why We Need the Method Master

The Method Master understands that two things drive improved student learning. The first is that successful schools have an effective and stimulating learning climate. This is why researchers of leadership theory spend considerable time investigating issues of culture and climate. If the environment is toxic, even with highly trained professionals involved, deep change is not likely to happen (Reason, 2010).

Second, we understand that high-performing schools consistently use research-based instructional methods and develop a systemic expectation that instructional methodology matters and is always evolving. The Method Master embodies these expectations and knows that schools cannot significantly influence student learning unless they continue to bring state-of-the-art innovation to their current learner-ready instructional strategies.

If learning is the most important outcome of our efforts in schools, then we need Method Masters to improve upon what we know about developing instructional strategies that elicit the very best learning outcomes for the students we serve.

The Method Master: Advantages and Benefits

They Own the Best Tools and Share Their Tools With Others

The Method Master is known for maintaining great depth and breadth of knowledge regarding instructional methods. Colleagues know that when they have children with difficult learning challenges, the Method Master has access to the best tools available to diagnose and respond to the learning challenge. The Method Master understands it isn't enough to gather the best tools and apply them here and there. Indeed, Method Masters must demonstrate a willingness to consistently share their tools with teaching colleagues in their school and beyond.

They Are Willing to Own the Results of the Instructional Change Process

Method Masters take seriously the art and science of instruction. They are also quick to monitor their results and own the outcomes. Because they are the experts when it comes to instruction, they recognize their responsibility for student achievement outcomes.

The work of these teacher leaders is especially challenging when dealing with a child from a difficult home environment, chaotic community circumstances, or possessing other risk factors. In these cases, their efforts in providing outstanding instructional experiences will be key in determining the type of results they achieve.

School improvement research reveals that ownership of school improvement results is an important component in initiating meaningful and sustainable change (Fullan, 2001). As a result, the Method Master becomes a powerful figure in leading change. And they believe the change starts with them.

They Use Their Expertise to Keep Everyone Honest

Truth be told, the debate over school improvement approaches is often driven by gut-level emotional responses rather than a best-practice analysis of current and potential outcomes. Method Masters, however, are ultimately loyal to the research and tend to see these dramatic emotional ebbs and flows as a distraction to their objective of always identifying the best way forward.

When a school improvement team seeks a change in student performance, Method Masters provide thoughtful reflection on pathways toward improvement based on data, research, and a practiced sensibility about steps to take to stimulate improved learning. This dedication to research and craft helps Method Masters keep their teaching colleagues honest and allows them to advocate for school change in an authentic way.

LOOKING IN THE MIRROR: BECOMING THE METHOD MASTER

Please consider your existing mental models as they relate to the teacher leader as Method Master. Try to evaluate your teaching practice according to this scale quickly. This will provide you an honest look at yourself in relation to this type of teacher leadership.

Discussion of Classroom Applications

The Method Master understands that not everything we know from the past is wrong. Longstanding teacher practices will likely continue to be effective in the classroom. The Method Master is enough of a scientist to be open to the possibility that future learners could bring unique challenges that require dramatically different approaches. Like a doctor who

Classroom Applications for the Method Master

Old Reflection		*New Reflection*
Tried and true methods continue to work.	5 4 3 2 1 0 1 2 3 4 5 ←→	Each generation of learners brings new challenges. Our tried and true methods may not continue to work.
This is how I teach. It is my style.	5 4 3 2 1 0 1 2 3 4 5 ←→	This is how I teach. My approach matches the learning needs of this particular group of students.
I do not read educational or related research. These "scientists" are out of touch.	5 4 3 2 1 0 1 2 3 4 5 ←→	I am consistently reading educational and related research. These scientists give me clues to the steps I can take to improve instruction.

must be open to the possibility that longstanding cures may no longer work, the Method Master is steadfastly aware of what has worked in the past while remaining open to adopting new approaches.

There continues to be a focus on how teachers teach rather than strategically diagnosing the learning needs of students and applying instructional strategies. The shift away from what teachers are doing to what students are learning is at the heart of what Method Masters accomplish.

The Method Master will be a leader in helping schools move away from negative perceptions of research. What we need instead is a deeper understanding of scientific innovations in learning and how these breakthroughs can help teachers reach more students in an effective manner.

Schoolwide Change for the Method Master

Old Reflection		*New Reflection*
The principal and/or central office defines our training needs and guides us in keeping up with the best teaching methods.	5 4 3 2 1 0 1 2 3 4 5 ⟷	The teachers are on the front line of acknowledging, studying, and adopting best-practice teaching methods.
When teachers get experience and tenure, they can then provide meaningful input on best practice.	5 4 3 2 1 0 1 2 3 4 5 ⟷	When new teachers arrive, they are immediately given the opportunity to provide meaningful input on best practice.
The secrets to school improvement are getting a new principal, adopting a new schedule, getting a new book, and updating the curriculum.	5 4 3 2 1 0 1 2 3 4 5 ⟷	The secrets to school improvement will be the consistent adoption and application of state-of-the-art instructional methods in our school.

Discussion of Schoolwide Change

When it comes to change, there is far too much focus on what is happening in the principal's office as opposed to what is happening in the classroom. Political struggles over who said what and who is in charge don't typically result in improved student achievement. Teachers almost universally acknowledge that in the teachers' lounge and other informal collaborative spaces, teachers spend more time focused on the principal and his or her actions than the specifics of what is happening in the classroom.

Looking back at twentieth-century schools, teachers were deliberately isolated, affording principals the opportunity to have the best access to information and knowledge about school issues and processes. This isolation allowed administrators to control the flow of information and become the focus in times of change.

The idea of a teacher leader as Method Master, however, shifts the focus and puts teachers in control of how they instruct. Since teachers are ultimately closest to the work, it stands to reason that they should make the decisions that shape what happens in their classroom.

Strategies for Becoming and Supporting the Method Master

Teaching is not just a feel-good profession that anyone can practice because they care about kids and are willing to try hard. Stimulating learning is an art and a science and requires the mastery of the craft of teaching. Besides being driven by the desire to have a positive impact on the learning process, successful teachers must understand essential research methods and approaches (Bapuji & Crossan, 2004).

While we may collectively agree that this is an important sensibility, we believe that future teacher leaders will embrace the role of Method Master as a means to professionalizing instructional practice in a real and visceral way. You have undoubtedly known teachers whose professionalism seemed to emanate from everything they did. To promote the presence of this sensibility in schools, we recommend the following strategies.

Instructional Methods

Reflection Time Strategy

Today, we celebrate the emerging popularity of professional learning communities. The idea that professionals can come together and improve their individual and team performance is one we hope will not just come and go with other educational trends. But we also hope that educators will not forget the merits of individual reflection about their own professional practice.

Most of us take time in one way or another to think back on the work we do in school. Perhaps your reflection time is in your car on the way home, or at moments between grading papers, or during your planning period. We recommend that you discipline yourself to individualized reflection regarding your own instructional methods. Set time aside to look at the data, think about the work you did, and reflect on how your students responded to your efforts in the classroom.

Teachers often say it is difficult to find time for this type of reflection each day. If, however, our goal is to stimulate learning and our strategies in the classroom differentiate the degree to which this happens, the investment in thinking about our performance is time well spent. The act of reflection, after all, individually and collectively, helps to stimulate the learning process and can lead to deeper levels of understanding (Cohen & Robertson, 2007).

We also recommend that during your individualized reflection, you resist the temptation to simply plot out the next day's lesson or strategize about some mid-range goal. Instead, get deeply reflective about the instructional strategies you used. Did you use what you know about best practice and implement this strategy in class today? Were there key steps that you left out? What could you have done to maximize what you know about this approach?

By investing in deep thinking about your current practice, you may completely avoid challenges or setbacks you may have faced without such contemplation. Thus, the time you spend in thoughtful reflection will prepare you to deliver better results each day.

Agreed-Upon Institutional Best Practices Strategy

One of the most powerful things a school can do is to clarify its expectations for instructional best practice. What are the tenets of good lesson planning? What does a team believe about instruction, intervention, assessment, and so on? This can be a conversation that gets bogged down quickly with arguments and disagreements, even among highly successful teachers.

What we suggest is to start with a few baseline assumptions that everyone can accept as best instructional practices. Starting small and identifying three or four initial points of agreement open the lines of communication about best-practice methodology. It could become the starting point for professional development. It could be a talking point at faculty meetings. It could be a point of reflection in examining data points and evaluating strategies and approaches. Teacher leaders at the center of this discussion are exactly what is needed to own the process and its results. If this strategy is properly implemented, a guest should be able to enter a building and see what the institution stands for in relation to instructional practice.

All participants in this type of planning need to be clear that their work in this area is never done. Everyone must be dedicated to continuous improvement.

Celebrate and Share the Mastery Strategy

Teachers, administrators, and community members well beyond the boundaries of a local district may hear of a Method Master's advanced knowledge in a particular area. These teacher leaders often speak at state conferences, write white papers related to instructional strategies, and lead training of other teachers. Teacher leaders should encourage colleagues to develop an expertise strong enough to share at the state or national level.

Sending teachers to conferences continues to be an expensive endeavor. With the advent of blogs and other virtual communication spaces, however, teachers can express their knowledge in ways that will potentially reach even more people, and bring learning opportunities from afar.

We recommend that schools make it a consistent practice to identify Method Masters, teachers who can represent the school with their expertise in methodology, and look for venues to promote their work. This can obviously be of great assistance in furthering the careers of those involved, encouraging teachers to accelerate their development, and even recruiting new teachers to the school in hopes of joining an illustrious team of Method Masters.

Laboratory Classrooms Strategy

Just as blacksmiths allow apprentices to observe their craft, Method Masters are eager to share insights and strategies with colleagues by inviting them into their classrooms, as well as being guests in theirs. With curiosity as a driving force, they are willing to observe and be observed. They then spend time picking the brains of other professionals who can reflect on the progress of the students they serve. Method Masters understand that observing one another is an extremely important part of the learning process (Armantier, 2004). When you observe and reflect, opportunities to learn emerge for everyone involved.

Thus, the true mark of Method Masters is their willingness to teach other teachers and to learn from them. The key here is to take this idea and formalize it. Having a rotating laboratory classroom, for example, wherein teachers agree to drop in on one another in a systematic way can create this experience. It may even encourage teachers to try new techniques and ask colleagues to observe.

Establishing laboratory classroom observation opportunities in a departmental schedule can bring the idea of observation and reflection to fruition. By scheduling these types of activities, the emergence of more Method Masters is encouraged.

Process Reflection Strategy

Teachers have always known intuitively that learning is best demonstrated when students must articulate their thinking in arriving at their answer or decision. The memory process is driven by the capacity to literally reconstruct in our brains those episodes in the past (Koenig & Mecklinger, 2008).

Recognizing this, Master Methodologists approach the improvement of methodology by articulating their thinking process in applying their craft. So, Method Masters explain the methods they use, articulate why they use them, and reflect aloud as to how that best strategy worked on the learning activity. This ability to articulate the process and rationale helps the Method Master make thoughtful decisions about instruction and refine and improve on that process.

The process of reflecting aloud can be practiced with trusted colleagues, or perhaps within a professional journal in which instructors record what they accomplished and their reflections on the learning process. Method Masters must be process oriented and aware of their thinking while making key decisions related to enhancing student learning.

One way to implement the process reflection strategy is to build time into faculty meetings for this type of reflection. Organizing teachers into dyads and directing them to come prepared to reflect on a specific aspect of their teaching will help demonstrate the organization's commitment to reflection and collaboration.

If this type of opportunity isn't available, teacher teams within the school can make the decision to set aside time to reflect together. While this may seem to take time away from the business of the day, these opportunities to reflect invariably lead to new levels of understanding that improve our performance in both the short and long run.

Selective Abandonment Strategy

Just as a dentist may need to discard a favorite but antiquated piece of equipment, a Method Master understands that just because a particular method worked twenty years ago, doesn't mean it will necessarily continue to do so.

The field of education is often accused of having a cluttered agenda. Teacher leaders understand that part of the solution is being willing to give up one thing to embrace another. Method Masters don't, however, discard methods without being thoughtful about their rationale and the advantages of their decision. But when new tools become available and they are convinced of their effectiveness, Method Masters aren't afraid to retire the approaches of the past.

The act of selective abandonment can be done individually, perhaps when a teacher reflects on his or her own professional practice. It also can be a shared activity wherein teachers meet prepared to discuss strategies they feel they have outgrown and are willing to leave behind. This type of discussion can be cathartic and give teachers the courage to try new things, to push beyond what might be limiting beliefs.

Methods-Based Hiring Strategy

In job interviews, it is easy to get caught up in personality. Charming candidates make us feel comfortable in an interview setting and their ability to connect with us may fool us into believing they will make the same connection in the classroom. When hiring new teachers, priority should be placed on the candidate's knowledge of instructional methodologies and the tools he or she will use to articulate an extraordinary level of command in the classroom.

Being a Method Master requires a personality that connects with students, but we can no longer afford to hire a well-intentioned, friendly teacher who is not tuned in to the instructional methods that make a difference in student learning. New candidates we hire should reveal a strong knowledge of pedagogy and a well-articulated set of instructional strategies ready to be applied in the classroom. If a candidate comes to the interview with very few tools in their toolbox, it may be a sign that he or she is ill prepared to teach and is relying on personality instead.

To make sure that instructional competence is demonstrated at the very beginning, the human resources department or the interview team should insert it as a hiring criterion to ensure it is part of the exploration for the right candidate.

Instructional Methods in PLCs Strategy

In schools implementing professional learning communities (PLCs) as recommended by DuFour (2004), one focus will certainly be ongoing developments in instructional methodology. Schools, if necessary, should be reminded to give teachers time in various collaborative venues to reflect on instructional methodology and to address the steps they can take to continue to enhance their craft.

When these opportunities to reflect on and discuss instructional methodologies are made available, they emphasize the importance of this aspect of the profession. They also help ferret out those approaches that are effective as well as those that have outlived their usefulness.

Teaching Methods Study Group Strategy

Throughout this text, we have discussed the advantages of pulling together study groups from local, state, national, and international sources and establishing collegial conversations around specific topics. Teacher leaders who are Method Masters particularly enjoy the process of collaborating with colleagues on methodology topics, especially when the conversation can potentially enhance their evolution in the profession.

Principals and teacher leaders can initiate study teams to examine particular issues in methodology, and then actively seek out experts to join the conversation. With today's technology, such exchanges are not limited geographically and can be continued over a long period of time.

Publicize the Method Master Strategy

Many principals or groups of teacher leaders produce a monthly, quarterly, or annual publication that describes what is happening in the organization. Why not produce a feature about the school's Method Masters and describe the impact they have in the classroom. The article could include a description of their specific approaches, the steps they take to master the methodologies they implement, and the lengths they go in preparing themselves for this level of work.

One benefit of featuring instructional strategies or methods in publications is that it helps bring credibility to the profession. It can also showcase the professionalism of teachers for the community, parents, and anyone else who reads the publication.

Teachers have historically been underappreciated for the excellence they demonstrate in the classroom. They have toiled for too many years without enough recognition due to the isolated nature of the job itself. Bringing this important aspect of what it means to be a teacher into focus helps to create more respect and recognition for the teaching professional.

Venture Capital for Learning Innovation Strategy

If a school district decides a certain approach to instruction is important to pursue, it might consider setting aside an allotment of funding to serve as *venture capital* for learning innovation. Ideally, these funds would be disseminated by a team of representative teacher leaders who are interested in supporting the advancement of a particular learning innovation.

Those familiar with the concept of venture capital understand that it is designed to provide funding for the exploration of creative ideas or innovations. While in business, venture capital funding may help a small business deliver an exciting innovation to the market, in a local school district, a small amount of funding may go a long way in supporting a creative group of teachers in exploring an instructional innovation that could improve learning.

In most cases, when districts experiment with this type of strategy, the funding itself isn't as significant as the creativity that is sparked by the teachers who disseminate the funds and those "venture capitalists" who seek to experiment and evolve as leaders in the classroom.

"Go Ahead and Try" Strategy

In an effort to stimulate creativity, some schools have tried offering a fun and thoughtful "free pass" to allow teachers to experiment with a new approach in their classroom. The pass comes with an expectation that the recipients will report back to teaching colleagues and administrators regarding the creative approaches they took in honing their instructional practices. Even if the approach fails to meet its objectives, there is recognition that there will be forgiveness for what ostensibly becomes a good try.

The advantage of this strategy is that it creates a spirit of fun and experimentation in relation to teacher learning and thoughtfulness about methodologies. While improving teaching methods is serious business, it doesn't mean that the participants can't play a little along the way.

Furthermore, this type of free pass helps to create a sense of trust with administration. No one expects that teachers will get everything perfectly right the first time. But this strategy allows teachers to experiment without feeling that their attempts to be creative will be punished by the superiors who write their evaluations.

Transcendent Teacher Leaders in Action: The Method Master

Perhaps the best example of a Method Master from our profiles at the beginning of the book is Mary Ann. One of the main reasons Mary Ann developed credibility as a teacher was because she had the capacity to master cooperative learning as a preferred instructional method. What was magical about her performance in the classroom was that she did not rely on the method as her benchmark of success. Learning was what she was after and the cooperative learning method allowed her to stay focused on that outcome. Thus, Mary Ann's expertise in instructional methodology set her apart. Her excellence resulted in better learning for her students, a more prominent leadership voice with her colleagues and administration, and the capacity to shape the work of a generation of teachers who were inspired by her excellence and followed her lead.

Kate's love for her students was important, but she also needed sound instructional strategies in the area of reading to address the deficits her students brought with them. While her care and concern meant a lot to her students, her love alone would not prepare them for college. Instead, she realized that to serve her students she would have to apply a great deal of discipline and step out of her comfort zone in learning and applying these important instructional strategies in reading.

Over the last two decades, we have learned much about the brain, learning, and the specific steps we can take to stimulate growth and improve student achievement. In that time, our profession has become more complex and those teachers making an impact are the ones who continue to develop their skills throughout their careers. Any teacher today who is successful is operating to some degree as a Method Master. By focusing on this type of teacher leader, perhaps we can finally make the case that the highly technical work of being a teacher is a unique calling that takes high levels of skill and ability.

Conclusions

The notion that teacher leadership is driven to a great extent by a mastery of instructional methods is an idea that goes back to the work of a number of previous scholars in teacher leadership (Daggett, 2000). Today, we still need to maintain this fidelity to the ongoing development of best instructional practices in the profession. Many of the challenges we face will be solved by the emotional drive of great teams of leaders forging ahead. They will need to be fortified by careful, thoughtful, and strategic applications of the best instructional methods available.

The image of the Method Master may not be completely novel to you. You may know teachers who have a stealth command of teaching methodologies that seem to flow effortlessly in shaping their learning environment each day. Unfortunately, teachers are often portrayed as solemn, solitary experts who toil alone in developing their expertise. In thinking about the Method Master, we see something a bit different. These teachers are certainly knowledgeable, but they're also fun, flexible, and ready to share. While they probably have the answers, they're willing to ask others for help and perspective. They know their job is never ending and they are willing to be both teacher and student when working with others and honing their craft. There are undoubtedly Method Masters in your school waiting to emerge and to take the lead in this all-important area. Is this type of teacher leadership in your mirror in the morning?

The toolbox utilized for the Method Master represents to us the open minds of these teacher leaders. They desire to remain open in their never-ending search for new tools that will inform their practice and help the teachers they work with improve theirs, too. We hope that as you visualize this toolbox, you continue to gather the best methods possible and make your journey a public one, allowing others to gaze into your collection and borrow and share as needed. As you develop your expertise, we hope you recognize the growing number of tools available to you and help others to expand their collections as well.

7

The Fully Invested Owner

Take pride in your work at all times. Remember, respect for an umpire is created off the field as well as on.

—Ford Frick

The Fully Invested Owner Defined

Fully Invested Owners aren't dabbling in teaching; they are all in. They recognize the stakes are high and that each day in the classroom represents an opportunity to inspire and ignite the human potential. These leaders are invested in "their" students, "their" colleagues, and "their" school and they feel all the joys and pains associated with true ownership and responsibility. They have a long-term focus and resist being distracted by short-term struggles. Their humble classroom is sacred ground to them. When they walk into school each day, they find a part of themselves. They are the school. Like a tree, Fully Invested Owners' roots grow deeper and stronger each year while their branches reach ever higher.

Why We Need the Fully Invested Owner

Schools that play the blame game are not capable of instituting meaningful change. There are many schools where the principal blames the teachers, the teachers blame the parents, and everyone blames the students. When an ownership mentality is missing, arguments ensue about the division of labor and the placement of fault. In an era when technology allows information to pass so quickly, schools that lack an ownership mentality promulgate blame and division even faster.

Fully Invested Owners believe that deep change is their job and spend their days seeking solutions and innovation rather than blame. Thus, an ownership mentality is more important than ever and teacher leaders who become Fully Invested Owners will have an even greater impact moving forward.

The Fully Invested Owner: Advantages and Benefits

They Keep the Focus on Long-Term and Sustainable Changes

Teacher leaders who are Fully Invested Owners want solutions. Short-term solutions that may appeal during the latest political swing, the next round of negotiations, or a particular political season are of little interest to Fully Invested Owners. They recognize that deep and significant change takes a long time and they believe in staying constant to the values, ideas, and beliefs that matter most to them.

If the Fully Invested Owner supports a change initiative, he or she is going to expect everyone involved to take a similar long-term perspective. Fully Invested Owners bring deep thinking and sustainability to the change process. They may be slower at times to buy into change because of their desire to choose carefully. If and when they do buy in, however, they will seek to lead in such a way that principals and fellow teachers will be motivated to make a similar investment of themselves in the change process.

The research on deep, systemic change in schools and beyond has consistently held that organizations are much more effective when they maintain a long-term view of what they are trying to accomplish (Harackiewicz, Barron, Tauer, Carter, & Elliot, 2000). Part of the role of the Fully Invested Owner is to help colleagues keep those larger aspirations in mind when driving change and resist being swept away by what might be episodic bumps in the road.

They Lead Without Conditions

Schools that lack an ownership mentality often discuss potential change initiatives with a long list of qualifying conditions introduced as precursors to any attempts at deep change. For example, they may claim that if the school had better hiring policies, a better principal, or a more competent community, board, and superintendent, deep change at the building level might indeed be possible.

Unfortunately, what this leads to is the collective expectation that unless conditions are perfect, deep change isn't possible. While the most successful school districts have all of these conditions in alignment, teacher leaders who are Fully Invested Owners understand that waiting for that moment of perfection could take a lifetime. Things are seldom perfect and the Fully Invested Owner would rather attempt to lead significant change in imperfect conditions than wait for the stars to align before they take any action.

Thus, these ownership-oriented teacher leaders know that the only way significant progress is possible is to forge ahead with the hand they've been dealt. In many respects, this willingness is rewarded with the emergence of unexpected levels of excellence in a condition-free environment.

They Pursue Data While Keeping Students in Mind

School personnel know how important it is to gather the right data sets and reflect on them comprehensively in the name of long-term school improvement (Bernhardt, 2009). We expect that in years to come, this focus on data will continue to evolve as our data-gathering mechanisms improve. That said, however, the Fully Invested Owner recognizes that the pursuit of data is not the end in and of itself. Instead, the data gathered should be a reminder of the attempts we make each day to serve individual learners.

While aggregate reports help us understand trends, deeply impactful teacher leaders who are Fully Invested Owners know that there are names, faces, and heartfelt aspirations with each child that makes up the data sets on a spreadsheet. Since school is home to the Fully Invested Owner, it is important to remind ourselves that the data we gather is a reflection of the individual efforts of each student we serve. The Fully Invested Owner is a teacher leader who will make that connection and should be encouraged to share it whenever possible. Reflecting on an individual student helps make the pursuits real and the trend analysis more impactful.

They Play the Role of Reflective Historian

While the Fully Invested Owner isn't necessarily the teacher with the most experience, this type of teacher leader often develops over an extended period of time in a school and grows to understand what it means to work there. While new principals may arrive ready to lead a local renaissance, the Fully Invested Owner understands where the school has been, the struggles that might lie ahead, and the strategies that might lead to the deepest levels of change. In a culture in which we are so quick to reinvent or replace old conventions, the Fully Invested Owner leads this evolution with caution and the ability to reflect thoughtfully on triumphs and defeats of the past.

Do not be mislead by the role of reflective historian and miscategorize this teacher leader as someone living in the past. Like any good historical scholar, Fully Invested Owners have the ability to accurately reflect on the past, pointing out both its brilliance and its ineptitude.

This is why many Fully Invested Owners approaching the end of their careers may become advocates of change. At this point, they can thoughtfully reflect on perhaps decades of well-intentioned attempts at change that have not resulted in the type of reform they hoped for. Just because deep change has not happened in the past, however, doesn't mean this type of teacher leader isn't capable of being part of a successful change effort in the future.

They Help Develop a More Courageous and Empowered Environment

Two of the greatest sources of poor performance in schools are feelings of fear and lack of ownership (Wood, Norris, Waters, & Stoldt, 2008). When teachers are never given the opportunity to work on resolving their problems, they struggle on a number of levels.

First, when they don't own the solutions, they don't learn to own the problem at a depth that generates a desire to find creative solutions. This serves to weaken the creative energies that might otherwise be available to these teachers had they been empowered and ready to learn.

Second, one of the most uncomfortable feelings we experience as human beings is a lack of control. When we don't have control over our environment and change happens "to us" instead of "with us," our level of fear and uncertainty escalates and our ability to respond likewise diminishes.

A school teeming with teacher leaders who are Fully Invested Owners can overcome these feelings and create an environment that owns its challenges and solutions, learns to become more creative, and feels much less stress and fear because they know that they will be a part of the long-term solutions.

Looking in the Mirror: Becoming the Fully Invested Owner

We would like you to once again consider your existing mental models as they relate to the teacher leader as Fully Invested Owner. Try to evaluate your teaching practice according to this

Classroom Applications for the Fully Invested Owner

Old Reflection		*New Reflection*
I blame the system.	5 4 3 2 1 0 1 2 3 4 5 ←→	I am the system.
This is the place that I work.	5 4 3 2 1 0 1 2 3 4 5 ←→	This is *my* school.
A bad principal can ruin a good school.	5 4 3 2 1 0 1 2 3 4 5 ←→	A bad principal can be a formidable hurdle in our journey as teachers.
When will the (board of education, principal, parents, etc.) get busy and fix this problem?	5 4 3 2 1 0 1 2 3 4 5 ←→	What can we do about this problem? How soon can we get started?

scale quickly. This will provide you an honest look at yourself in relation to this type of teacher leadership.

Discussion of Classroom Applications

We are not the only profession that finds comfort in placing blame. While it may provide temporary and cathartic release to identify all the hurdles we must face to make a difference, every teacher reading this book can recognize that quiet voice inside that we hear every time we make this kind of excuse. From looking at the list on the right, it is clearly much more difficult to admit that we are the system, that the school is ours, or that even with a less-effective principal, we can make progress.

Discussion of Schoolwide Change

In looking at these questions related to schoolwide change, it is clear that teacher leaders who are Fully Invested Owners are willing to own major aspects of the change process and are even willing to reach out and lend their support in areas that

Schoolwide Change for the Fully Invested Owner

Old Reflection		*New Reflection*
The principal is really struggling. I wonder what he or she will do.	5 4 3 2 1 0 1 2 3 4 5 ←→	The principal is really struggling. What should we do?
The test scores are low. What if the tests, kids, parents, and so on were different?	5 4 3 2 1 0 1 2 3 4 5 ←→	The test scores are low. What if we as a team were different? How can we make it better?
How many days before the weekend? How soon before the next break? How soon before I retire?	5 4 3 2 1 0 1 2 3 4 5 ←→	How much more can I contribute? What is left to give?

may be out of their control. For example, in exploring the role of teachers in relation to a struggling principal, we have found that in far too few cases are teachers willing to step up and help that principal. When reflecting on such a situation, however, most groups of teachers agree that their individual or collective support could go a long way in helping the principal be successful. Furthermore, most teachers agree that a successful principal makes their work in the classroom more enjoyable and their opportunities to lead change more likely. The ownership mentality of teacher leaders who are Fully Invested Owners helps to stimulate willingness to reach out and support principals when that additional help is needed.

This is also true when reflecting on test scores. While there are a number of factors that go into student performance on assessments, it is clear that teachers make a difference and teacher leaders who are Fully Invested Owners are ready to own their portion of the success or failure of their students.

We presented the third question in this section because we have found over the years that there are far too many highly qualified, influential teachers who are poised to make different levels of contribution based on where they see themselves in their career. For example, we have known teachers who elected not to be part of a change process because they were only two or three years from retirement. Perhaps this is due in part to the fact that our profession has been measured to such a great extent by time that we pay an inordinate amount of attention on years earned and the days and months spent before a vacation or the end of a school year. That said, teacher leaders who develop an ownership mentality know they can make significant contributions right up until their last moments before a vacation or the last days of their career. The best teachers we've known never run out of the ability to make contributions, both small and large. They simply run out of time.

Strategies for Becoming and Supporting the Fully Invested Owner

Many scholars of teacher leadership have agreed over the years that maintaining an ownership orientation can have a powerful impact on school improvement (Smith-Burke, 1996). This section offers some specific, action-oriented strategies that teachers can use to move from just thinking about this concept to actually making it a part of who they are in their journey in teacher leadership.

Own the Space Strategy

There are many teachers who find themselves playing the Hokey Pokey in their school. They put one foot in, yet keep one foot out. They never really move all the way in and fully commit to investing in their school. While this is an emotional decision that requires trust and a desire to give, teacher leaders who become Fully Invested Owners are willing to take that risk.

These teacher leaders are the ones who take whatever office or desk space the school gives them and immediately make it their own. They decorate it with personal effects or pictures and memorabilia that represent who they are as people and professionals.

Those of us who are too guarded to give of ourselves that way aren't likely to get in return the emotional connection we need to be fully invested. Think about how rented cars or homes are treated versus those that are owned and prized. There is a difference. Pride of ownership means extra levels of time and attention in caring for the investment.

When applying the Own the Space Strategy, it is important to establish a connection with your teaching space with some degree of caution. Some teachers have made the mistake of presenting too much of themselves personally in their classroom or on social networking spaces and have suffered enormous consequences.

Teacher leaders who are Fully Invested Owners recognize that their mission is to engage the deepest levels of learning in the students they serve and they make appropriate choices about what they share. This requires a certain professional sensibility that isn't easy to quantify. We all have many aspects of our personalities and teacher leaders share those aspects of their lives that help demonstrate their engagement and reinforce their mission when working with students.

So, teachers should move into their school work spaces and treat them as their own. Personalize those spaces so that students know you have moved in. Think of it as putting your stake in the ground. This is your sacred ground!

Own the Mission Strategy

The teaching profession can be a lot of fun. Those who love teaching laugh harder and more often than most professionals given the brilliance and absurdity of the children we serve. However, focused teacher leaders understand that, in the end, they are on a serious mission with life-changing consequences and time with each student is fleeting. These teachers know that if they can significantly influence the lives of their students, they truly are changing their corner of the world.

True teacher leaders don't see this as hyperbole. Instead, they recognize they must own their mission if they are to achieve the goals they desire. They must demonstrate that ownership mentality on a consistent basis. Helping a school culture develop teacher leaders who have a great adherence to an ownership mentality will be easier if the deepest, most profound mission is put forth consistently.

Teachers and other school leaders should frequently reintroduce the notions of mission and vision to the school to communicate the consequences of the work being done every day. A mission will not come to fruition without ownership and ownership cannot be stimulated without consistently reminding everyone why they come to work each day.

Adopt the "Us" Strategy

There continues to be an us-versus-them mentality in the field of education. We recognize that this focus on blame rather than mission ultimately degrades our energies and diminishes our capacity to lead significant levels of change (Mayers & Zapeda, 2002). We tend to heap blame the most at times when tension, confusion, and frustration are at their highest. It is precisely at these moments, however, that we should be blaming less and coming together more. We often do just the opposite.

If you are a teacher reading this book, you probably associate the us-versus-them mentality with teachers versus administration and have undoubtedly witnessed administrators get blamed when times get tough. Furthermore, administrators have also been known to blame teachers in the face of the same frustration, fear, and confusion.

The Fully Invested Owner recognizes that in an era with so many difficult challenges and complexities emerging at every level, it is extremely important to break the habit of blame. Ownership-oriented teacher leaders understand that an unsuccessful administration will result in stress and frustration for everyone.

In deeply divided schools, the challenge of serving students is even more difficult. But Fully Invested teacher leaders are confident enough in themselves, their abilities, and their capacity to shape their world to step forward and own their piece of the problem, process, and solution. They know that us versus them in the end will impact the bottom line and that it is more efficient and less stressful to face our challenges as "us."

Through the years, we have worked with schools where there was great division between principals and teachers. Not surprisingly, the principals in these schools wind up being unsuccessful and unfulfilled in their jobs. In these divided and toxic environments, it is easy to inspire conversations about "what's wrong with them?" It is difficult, however, to elicit steps anyone took to try to make things better for "us."

It might help to assign a staff member to monitor local conversations to see how often school personnel play the blame game. Principals and teachers alike can fall into this habit and it might help to have a thoughtful conversation on this topic. Such openness and honesty could inspire greater levels of participation. Scheduling it and bringing some formality to examining this issue will help change the outcomes in the school and increase levels of ownership behavior.

Appreciating Assets Strategy

We are consistently reminded that it is important to invest in appreciating, rather than depreciating, assets. For example, the purchase of a car is considered depreciating because it is worth less each moment that we own it. And, although current market conditions challenge this assumption, investing in real estate is an appreciating asset in that it is worth more as time goes by. While there is no magic bullet when it comes to investing, it's clear that to some extent the best investors are those who invest strategically within appreciating assets.

Teacher leaders who are Fully Invested Owners, like any good investor, are interested in making consistent and long-term investments in appreciating assets. They don't mind toiling for many years if they believe that the conditions are right for improved levels of success. They hope to consistently invest their energies and expertise in those thoughtful habits and ideas that can be sustained over a long period of time and will have a cumulative impact and improve the school over time.

The teacher leader as Fully Invested Owner is also smart enough not to panic when their investment may be in jeopardy, nor do they overreact at an opportunity that seems too good to be true. They know that over a long period of time, a habit of focused and steady investment in appreciating assets always leads to better outcomes.

To make this strategy real, school leaders might consider setting time aside to reflect on how their ownership mentality has resulted in better outcomes for their students. It can be something as simple and cathartic as identifying those points of pride in the school where outcomes are steadily getting better.

When we step back to reflect on the merits of our actions and the rewards we get from owning our results, there is a sense of community celebration, a good feeling about what emerges that makes us want to repeat those steps moving forward. Building this type of appreciation into our reflection time can help with this strategy.

Ceremony and Tradition Strategy

Ceremony and tradition are beloved yet misunderstood aspects of the school experience. The reason ceremony and tradition are so important is that they tend to elicit an intense emotional connection to the circumstance or event at hand. We know that emotion has a huge impact on learning, and tradition and ceremony are keys to stimulating engagement and creating a climate of connection and learning.

We have not, however, been as strategic about the use of ceremony and tradition as we should have been. In most schools, when you ask teams what they celebrate on an annual basis, the answers are often inconsistent at best. Many of the ceremonies have little to do with their most important missions and may be maintained at this point out of habit or obligation.

Principals and thoughtful teacher leaders who are interested in developing ownership mentality should initiate and maintain ceremonies and traditions relating to the school's most important objectives. If outstanding instructional practices that stimulate deep learning are truly the school's raison d'être, then tradition, ceremony, and honors for that work should follow. By creating a consistent pattern of thoughtfully and respectfully celebrating and formally recognizing those most key elements in the school, we are more likely to develop an ownership mentality and see more of this type of behavior.

Does your school honor outstanding teaching? Does it honor outstanding service? Or have you fallen into the trap of placing the most dramatic rewards on those who are retiring or leaving the school? While we do want to honor those who are leaving the institution, this sends the interesting message that the greatest recognition for a teacher comes when they leave. A deeper sense of ownership would be developed if those rewards came a bit sooner.

Promote Ownership in Others Strategy

Principals and prominent teacher leaders are often highly skilled and have the capacity to make tough decisions. Principals and teacher leaders alike must learn to give away the decision making power to allow others to learn to lead change on their own. A highly confident, ownership-oriented teacher leader did not get that way without trial and error.

The degree to which an organization is open to teachers making their own decisions and owning both the process and the results will dictate the degree to which this type of leadership will flourish. It is not easy for a principal or prominent teacher leader to step back and let a colleague struggle to make decisions that may not be ideal. It is with these types of experiences, however, that ownership emerges. We learn by doing and real-life situations allow teachers to expand their skills and grow as leaders.

There has been much written about the merits of empowering others and giving them authority in the change process and the positive results that emerge (Conger, 1989; Srivastava, Bartol, & Locke, 2006). This will clearly continue to be important for the next generation of teacher leaders.

Transcendent Teacher Leaders in Action: The Fully Invested Owner

Each of the teacher leaders profiled at the beginning of the book is a great example of a teaching professional who owns his or her journey at the deepest levels. Kate wasn't certified to teach the students she dedicated herself to serving. Her mission was so important to her that she took on the challenge anyway and found a way to be successful.

Khris's willingness to join her students in owning the job of supporting the learning needs of children living halfway around the world represents an awe-inspiring dedication to her mission. She not only demonstrated ownership in her own right, but was also able to convey the ownership mentality to her students and to countless friends, colleagues, and benefactors she engaged to bring this dream to fruition.

Jim attended to every detail in transforming his football program. The steps he took wouldn't necessarily fit in the job description for a football coach; but because his players and program became a part of who he was, he went above and beyond what was expected and achieved unusual effectiveness as a result.

Mary Ann also owned her classroom, her school, her methodologies, and her results. Her well-honed expertise emerged thanks to a tireless, multi-decade effort to dedicate herself to the students she loved, the school she came to embrace, and the profession that she called her own.

Would your school benefit if its teacher leaders were more fully invested in the students, school, each other, and the profession? What would a deeper sense of ownership do to job satisfaction in the school? How might it change the climate and impact how people work day-to-day with one another?

Conclusions

Each of us has undoubtedly faced those moments when we have to make a decision about the path we will commit to. While such a decision can be stressful, we also can identify with the relief we feel when the guesswork is over. We have committed and we are all in. Our brains no longer fumble with multiple options and instead can focus on maximizing the choice we made.

The Fully Invested Owner understands this feeling and can work in the teaching profession with the clarity and satisfaction that comes when we fully commit to something that is important to us. The Fully Invested Owner is a step ahead of those who don't commit because even though they may feel the stress of performing to their own high standard, they likewise feel the relief of choosing a path and sticking with it.

Perhaps in your journey to becoming a teacher you were shaped by a dedicated teacher or colleague along the way who owned their journey in a similar fashion to the illustrations we have provided in this chapter. If so, you are fortunate. We hope the image we have painted here has brought more clarity to what a Fully Invested Owner teacher leader is all about. After this exploration, do you see a Fully Invested Owner in your school? Do you see one in you?

For the Fully Invested Owner, we chose the image of a simple, small home neatly captured inside a circle. We hope that as you visualize yourself as a Fully Invested Owner, you remember that even a humble home is a beautiful destination if it's yours. Keep this humble, encircled home in mind as you continue to lay the foundation for your work in your school and make it your own.

8
The Present Balance Keeper

Balance, peace, and joy are the fruit of a successful life. It starts with recognizing your talents and finding ways to serve others by using them.

—Thomas Kinkade

The Present Balance Keeper Defined

The Present Balance Keeper is a teacher leader who understands that the challenges of the profession should inspire and engage, not engulf you. Teacher leaders understand the concept of time and they know that investments in themselves will allow them to serve others more effectively and for a longer period of time. Present Balance Keepers love teaching and are extremely devoted to their profession. They simultaneously remain well-rounded, well-read, and well traveled, and as a result bring a variety of experiences, side talents, and perspectives to their work as teachers. These teacher leaders know that having a variety of interests and maintaining a personal and professional balance makes them happier, healthier, and allows them to bring a fresh and empowered perspective to their work each day.

Why We Need the Present Balance Keeper

Being a Balance Keeper is more than being a good time manager. It is about staying connected with the most important demands in life, personally and professionally, and remembering to invest our energies in proportion to what is important. After all, each of us can relate to that internal nagging we feel when we know that our lives are out of balance. If we are devoting too much or too little energy to different portions of our lives, our internal sensibility tells us that we are out of balance. When this happens, we don't accomplish our goals as quickly as we would like.

Physical and natural law remind us that balance is the secret to speed, power, and momentum. A semi truck loaded improperly will grind out its wheels and tip over. Elite athletes won't break any speed records if their movements are not synchronized and in balance. Successful people in all walks of life demonstrate the capacity to maintain a balance in life and help others to do the same. This is the mission of the Present Balance Keeper.

When we are balanced, we have a better chance of spending time and devoting mental and emotional resources in the areas of our lives that matter. Additionally, the Present Balance Keeper recognizes that appropriate and focused levels of rest and diversion are key to staying happy and maintaining a clear perspective.

Neurologically speaking, we tend to learn more both individually and collectively when we have variety and occasional breaks from the normal grind. This is why study breaks have proven to be helpful. When we work or study for twenty or twenty-five minutes and take a break, our perspective as we resume work is better because our brain has had a chance to pull back and then become engaged again. This process has been shown to increase neurological stimulation (Cohen & Robertson, 2007).

While the Present Balance Keeper may be aware of the scientific impact of taking a break or having some downtime, they seem to know intuitively when everyone needs a break so that they can all come back to work with a fresh perspective. Given the hectic, rigorous challenges of schools today, this capacity to know when to stop is increasingly important and the Present Balance Keeper is a teacher leader who can lead the way.

The Present Balance Keeper: Advantages and Benefits

They Are Willing to Try New Things

The Present Balance Keeper understands the simple physics lesson that objects in motion tend to stay in motion, the definition of momentum. When it comes to momentum, the teacher leader as Present Balance Keeper knows you can never get too comfortable. You must strive constantly for new approaches, thoughts, and ideas.

Scanning the landscape for growth opportunities, Present Balance Keepers have a longstanding tradition of shedding practices, viewpoints, and approaches that aren't working and replacing them with new tools better suited to move forward. This openness does not mean that Present Balance Keepers will try absolutely anything. In fact, once equilibrium is established, it is their role to maintain that balance.

So, even though Present Balance Keepers are open to new opportunities, they also know that a delicate balance can be disrupted if the wrong approaches are adopted. This may sound contradictory, but Present Balance Keepers know how to walk this line. These teacher leaders understand that, even if their team is succeeding, there are always additional strategies lurking that could lead to new levels of improvement. Even if they are moving forward at a comfortable pace, finding the right strategy could lead to unprecedented levels of success. So, even if they are doing a good job, these teacher leaders are always willing to challenge the status quo.

Present Balance Keepers also recognize that a new idea could compromise current levels of progress. The fear of losing current momentum can keep teachers from taking even the smallest steps forward. How many teachers have you known over the years that were unwilling to make even the slightest change? That unwillingness in many cases is rooted in the fear that change will curtail their modest level of productivity and keep them from performing even at these less-than-stellar levels.

It is the courageous, insightful Balance Keeper who recognizes that the fear of losing your balance is real and, when it comes to innovation, individuals and teams need to be thoughtful about what they add to the mix. Yet, these teacher leaders are wise enough to know that without constantly scanning the environment for new innovations, they can't possibly achieve new levels of success.

They Bring Out-of-the-Box Thinking to the Team

One of the challenges in the change process is the lack of extraordinary ideas. While in the past, schools offered institutional rewards for compliance to standards and following the rules, schools in the next generation will be successful in direct proportion to their ability to imagine and institute creative innovations. Creativity, therefore, will be at an even greater premium and the ability to lead this type of innovation will depend on teacher leaders like the Present Balance Keeper.

To see how Present Balance Keepers assist in this area, think about some of the most creative moments you've shared on highly productive teams or groups. Say a group is grappling with a difficult challenge and, in the moment, the team stumbles on a learning innovation. To experience these light bulb moments, the group must be operating in the present. If we're thinking about past or potential failures, it's difficult to be in the present. Present Balance Keepers, therefore, help lead innovations thanks to their ability to take advantage of a spontaneous opportunity and live in the moment.

Sometimes when teams have worked together for a long time, they become so immersed in the details of their challenges that they lose sight of the big picture. A myopic perspective may also emerge due to a lack of experiences in the world outside of education. Present Balance Keepers, with their personal/professional life balance, bring rich and varied experiences to their work. Their experiences enable them to present fresh ideas and allow the team to reinvent essential aspects of their work and the strategies they use.

They Consistently Capitalize on "Other" Skills

Because Present Balance Keepers have a life outside of teaching, it is likely they have skill sets and knowledge bases useful inside their school. Teachers who are well traveled, for example, can bring an eyewitness view of other lands to the lessons they teach. Knowledge of music and art adds style and flavor to the school, adding richness to the organizational climate. You never know when a Present Balance Keeper's skills and abilities might come in handy. They consistently contribute in unique and surprising ways.

They Keep the Past, Present, and Future in Context

As stated earlier, Present Balance Keepers understand the value of embracing the moment. If individuals or teams aren't present and fully aware of their current growth opportunities, creative innovations aren't likely to emerge. These teacher leaders recognize, however, that if a team gets together for some important brainstorming, a transcendent innovation may not always occur.

In fact, there are times when teams will fail in their attempts to resolve a challenge. When this happens, thoughtful Present Balance Keepers understand the value of keeping the future in mind. There are always new learning opportunities on the horizon. This ability to focus on the present with an eye on the future allows Present Balance Keepers to push for innovations today, be patient if they don't come as quickly as they'd like, and be optimistic about new learning possibilities for the future.

Present Balance Keepers are also thoughtful and reflective about the past without dwelling on it. You may be aware of teacher leaders who spend an inordinate amount of time reliving days gone by. Of course there are lessons to be learned from our history. Present Balance Keepers will thoughtfully reflect on the habits of the past as a means for better understanding the capacities of today and the possibilities of tomorrow.

So, for example, thoughtful Present Balance Keepers may recall wonderful successes the school has enjoyed over the past five or ten years. Rather than reliving those days, however, Present Balance Keepers attempt to identify the elements that led to those successes. Conversely, they may reflect about past failures, try to figure out what went wrong, and identify actions they can take today.

Our professional lives exist on a continuum. The Present Balance Keeper understands that it is extremely important to keep the past, present, and future in context and to take moments to appreciate where we are, where we've been, and where we are likely to go.

Looking in the Mirror: Becoming the Present Balance Keeper

Just as in previous chapters, we would like you to consider your existing mental models as they relate to the teacher leader as Present Balance Keeper. Try to evaluate your teaching practice according to this scale quickly without analyzing it too deeply. This will provide you an honest look at yourself in relation to this type of teacher leadership.

Discussion of Classroom Applications

In the examples above, we see quite a paradigm shift from the old resolutions to the new ones of the teacher leader as a Present Balance Keeper.

Classroom Applications for the Present Balance Keeper

Old Reflection		*New Reflection*
I don't have enough time for that in my classroom.	5 4 3 2 1 0 1 2 3 4 5 ◄——►	Time is an investment. I try to invest wisely with my students.
Once things change, I will be able to make a difference for the students I serve.	5 4 3 2 1 0 1 2 3 4 5 ◄——►	I have this moment right now to make a difference for the students I serve. And I will.
The kids in my classroom today are different from those just a few years ago. This is terrible.	5 4 3 2 1 0 1 2 3 4 5 ◄——►	The kids in my classroom today are different from those just a few years ago. This is progress.
I keep my outside interests private.	5 4 3 2 1 0 1 2 3 4 5 ◄——►	I share my outside interests with my students. They help shape how I teach.

Many conversations about school improvement reveal an obsession with time. We obsess about how it is used, our lack of it, and how its passage will somehow bring solutions. Thoughtful teacher leaders know, however, that change will never come without anticipating, planning, and preparing for it.

The Present Balance Keeper doesn't see evolution as a negative. Such a view is contradictory to the progress our species has made. Students, parents, and the world we live in have changed. The Present Balance Keeper understands that if we don't look for those points in progress now, we won't be able to help shape this evolution in a positive way.

Discussion of Schoolwide Change

When looking at broader issues related to schoolwide change, the Present Balance Keeper understands that there is

Schoolwide Change for the Present Balance Keeper

Old Reflection		*New Reflection*
I give everything to my job. I am too exhausted to invest in me.	5 4 3 2 1 0 1 2 3 4 5 ⟷	I take care of myself first so I can bring the best of me to my job.
My circle of friends is made up of teachers.	5 4 3 2 1 0 1 2 3 4 5 ⟷	I have a broad circle of friends. Their diversity makes me smarter.
I wonder what the future in our school will bring.	5 4 3 2 1 0 1 2 3 4 5 ⟷	I wonder what we will bring to the future of our school.
These new teachers coming up today aren't the same. I don't understand them.	5 4 3 2 1 0 1 2 3 4 5 ⟷	These new teachers coming up today will have a unique journey. I look forward to supporting them while I have the chance.

great value in the moment. Taking action may represent our most important moments to positively impact the future.

Every school can benefit from the insights of the Present Balance Keepers. These teacher leaders deliberately put themselves in diverse situations in hopes of coming back to the school with fresh perspectives to apply to the challenges of the day.

Strategies for Becoming and Supporting the Present Balance Keeper

Teacher leaders operating as Present Balance Keepers are outstanding role models for their students. They demonstrate the intellectual curiosity needed to pursue a variety of intellectual interests. This curiosity brings energy and passion to their learning pursuits. What follows is a list of strategies teachers can use to become a Present Balance Keeper in today's schools.

Personal Pursuits Strategy

The Present Balance Keeper refuses to live life in a boring and disengaged way. These teacher leaders have numerous outside interests and their experiences and life pursuits bring an interesting viewpoint to the learning process.

Think about the best teachers you had in school. It is likely they were the ones who told you about the year they spent backpacking across Europe after college. Or they might have had an odd job, such as driving a taxi in New York for a summer or an abiding interest in art, music, or architecture. Their discoveries, interests, or talents may have inspired you to follow in their footsteps or learn more about the world as a result of their journey.

While all professions could benefit from a workforce with diverse experiences, it is clear that teachers with a wide variety of life experiences enrich their colleagues and, perhaps more important, the students they serve. Teachers spend their day sharing, talking, and explaining the world around them.

Once you have had some diverse life experiences, you undoubtedly see the world through a different lens. When you live, work, or study with someone who has had this level of experience, the benefits are geometric and even if you haven't shared the experience, their perspectives help you learn, grow, and evolve. A well traveled and experienced Present Balance Keeper could spend their career sharing their perspectives with several decades of students, who are deeply enriched by this learning and can move forward themselves in shaping the world.

Multiple Perspectives Strategy

Present Balance Keepers seek out unique learning opportunities. They are open to learning about new perspectives and emerging issues. These teacher leaders read authors and bloggers they may not agree with to understand a multitude of perspectives. While they may not change their minds, they are aware that by being exposed to multiple perspectives, their level of engagement deepens and the likelihood that they will learn something new is increased (Zorn, Page, & Cheney, 2000).

As a result, Present Balance Keepers are always seeking to connect with teaching colleagues from different disciplines, different grade levels, and of different generations. Their colleagues, collaborators, and mutual learning partners may look, pray, and play differently than they do; but they are secure enough in themselves and their capacity to learn to actively seek these differentiated learning partners. While past generations may have seen efforts in promoting diversity as a humane or appropriate measure, the Present Balance Keeper knows that in addition to these benefits, it promotes greater levels of creativity, innovation and change.

The Present Balance Keeper doesn't limit his or her school connections to fellow teachers. In some of the most successful schools we have seen, social gatherings include teachers, administrators, secretaries, custodians, and aides, and if you were to join the party, you wouldn't be able to tell one from the other. This improves everyone's perspective and helps create a climate where deep change is possible. The Present Balance Keeper is key to creating this type of school culture.

Chapter 5 presented the Synergy Networking and Change Strategy, which suggests that school teams seek a diversity of outside input when approaching change. The Multiple Perspectives Strategy is similar. But this strategy is a more formative aspect of Present Balance Keepers in that they are always seeking multiple perspectives to better understand the context of their work and improve their ability to reflect on the past, the present, and the future.

Purposeful Debate Strategy

Teacher leaders as Present Balance Keepers like a good debate. They are clear about the difference between debate and argument, and they often engage their friends and colleagues in discussions designed to probe a particular thought or idea. The Present Balance Keeper may take a contrary position to further the discussion. They regard debate as a tool for learning and use it to broaden their already wide horizons.

To make this strategy work, teams throughout the school should engage in the debate process. Anyone who has studied debate knows that preparing a thoughtful presentation of ideas and cross-examining those concepts deepens your knowledge of the subject and may even change your mind.

One way to implement this strategy would be to pick a current change initiative at your school. Assign team members to one side or the other. After some preparation time, the first team argues for the change in an organized, point-by-point, timed fashion. The opposing team then argues against the change. They may address each point provided, presenting their counter-argument to each. This creates an organized and succinct discussion that allows all of the participants to engage directly with the issue at hand. Depending on the seriousness of the topic, the formality of such a debate may require more or less preparation.

There is value in getting teams to be thoughtful about what they're after and presenting an organized, cogent argument. It can ease the change process. It can allow teams to operate more in the present with less emotion. And it can result in a greater adherence to what we know about learning and change.

Reflect and Proceed Strategy

As mentioned earlier in the chapter, the Present Balance Keeper is willing to spend time in reflection, but doesn't believe in dwelling on the past. When ruminating past failures, our emotions are ignited and we find ourselves reliving those emotional states that were difficult to experience in the first place (Nolen-Hoeksema, 1991). Not only is it unhealthy for us to dwell on these negative emotions (Levenson, 2003), it also detracts from our capacity to profoundly reflect on the past and subsequently plan for the future.

Present Balance Keepers understand that their current and future practice will be improved when they thoughtfully reflect on their past professional experiences. Reflection is a key component to learning information in a way that allows it to be applied in a meaningful and authentic manner (Egorov, Unsicker, & von Bohlen, 2006). When we revisit and reflect on our professional experiences and retrace the steps we took to get there, we can direct future action toward our goals. The Present Balance Keeper reflects and does not dwell.

Formalizing the Reflect and Proceed Strategy is often most effective when dealing with what might be a systemic failure or letdown. For example, if test scores came back from the state and they were much lower than expected, it's important not to dwell on it if progress is to be made. But that doesn't mean the team's negative feelings should be ignored.

The time needed to process this type of disappointment is commensurate with the size of the failure. A major failure may take a longer time to process than a relatively minor one. Reflection is a necessity at times like this. Negative feelings must be purged or they will return later. Formalizing this step in the change process and making it part of how teams process change creates a greater degree of certainty that thoughtful innovation will occur. If teams actually schedule time for this type of pursuit, the benefits are much more likely to emerge.

Flexible View Forward Strategy

The teacher leader as Present Balance Keeper understands the future is never quite what we anticipate. The lesson plans for September 10, 2001, were probably quite different from those of September 12, 2001. No one could have predicted the events of 9/11, and the future no doubt will continue to surprise and change the work of teachers in the classroom.

Teacher leaders who are Present Balance Keepers plan for the future with this in mind. They know at any moment the outside world could bring unprecedented challenges and opportunities that could reshape their work in a significant way. These leaders keep their goals in mind and have a strategic plan for getting there. They are careful not to waste time with overplanning for a future that is likely to emerge quite differently from what anyone could have imagined.

It isn't easy finding the balance between being prepared for what's coming next while being flexible enough to respond to those changes that emerge. It's an imperfect science that is dependent on teacher leaders who can identify those most essential systemic outcomes and are clear from the onset as to where flexibility can be allowed and to what extent focus and rigidity may be necessary. Present Balance Keepers understand that being flexible and focused in their view of the future will make all the difference in their capacity to lead significant levels of change.

Capture the Moment Strategy

Arguably, the most important sensibility the teacher leader as Present Balance Keeper maintains is the ability to understand the power of the present. These teachers recognize that to be fully engaged with students, they must be as emotionally and mentally dialed in as possible. Minimizing obsessions with the past and future, they keep themselves in the moment, which allows them to be more responsive.

The advantage of staying in the present is that a teacher leader can take immediate steps to make a difference for a child. Say a teacher notices a child has a learning deficit. The Present Balance Keeper knows that addressing it now is just the right time. They don't hope that some future teacher will address the issue or that some other support will appear down the road. They understand that now may be the last chance for this student.

One way to infuse this strategy is to consistently ask the question, "What can we do right now?" When presented with a difficult school improvement challenge, the team may develop a long-term plan to help students over the next two or three years. However, in that thirty-six-month time period there will be a number of students who are not served. What can be done right now to help the students who aren't getting the service they need? Keeping a view on the future by consistently asking what we can do in the present helps remind us that every day on the job is important and every day offers us opportunities to make a difference.

Personal Wellness Strategy

We have discovered that learning at all levels is enhanced when learners are physically and emotionally fit (Cotman & Engessar-Cesar, 2003). Teacher leaders who represent the Present Balance Keeper allow time to take care of themselves physically and psychologically. Giving themselves time alone to debrief a situation will allow them to return with a healthier and more focused perspective. They also take care of their bodies because they know that it is the vessel with which they share their experiences and their lives. They know that neurologically, it is difficult for the brain to be at its optimal effectiveness if the body is unhealthy (Cotman & Engessar-Cesar, 2003).

Once again, committing themselves to keep their bodies fit is a strategy that teacher leaders may adopt on a personal level. Some schools have made this a team sport and come together to lose weight, get fit, and take care of themselves better. This helps to build community, add levels of effectiveness, and ultimately make us happier each day on the job.

Time and Energy Commitment Strategy

Present Balance Keepers tend to be able to get a lot done in a short period of time. They know how to manage their energies, can find their focus, and move forward rapidly. The reason they are strong in this area is that they are effective time managers who push through procrastination and resist overcommitment. Procrastination leads to a great deal of rushing around moving toward a deadline. It creates a certain frenetic energy that may pull our attention away from other endeavors, ultimately taking us out of balance.

Think about a time in college when you focused all your energy studying for one exam. It did little for your fitness level and you likely weren't very well prepared for any of your other classes that week. Well-intentioned teachers often become overcommitted and are unable to be effective in any aspect of their job. The newer we are to the profession, the more cautious we have to be regarding this issue and we must learn to gradually take on more as our talents and capacities evolve.

Transcendent Teacher Leaders in Action: The Present Balance Keeper

Each of the profiled teacher leaders in Chapter 1 had the capacity to understand the importance of taking advantage of the moment. They identified their challenges and acted quickly and decisively in making progress to their goals, even if that progress was slow or small to begin with.

Kate could have waited until another teacher was hired with the appropriate certification to lead the at-risk student intervention program she so skillfully created. Khris might have responded to the number of significant setbacks in her journey by simply waiting for them to pass or accepting "no" for an answer. Jim could have been satisfied with his team almost beating the state playoff contender that year and setting a foundation for better efforts in the future. Instead, he realized that all that mattered was that moment on that rainy night with the game on the line. Each of these leaders felt the urgency to act in the moment and had the vision to see the long-term implications of their momentary actions.

Each of these leaders was also advantaged by life experiences that were replete with opportunities to develop sidebar talents that shaped their journeys. Khris's international travel experiences certainly gave her insight into the world that she was able to draw on. Mary Ann's work in prison gave her a unique perspective on community and culture that shaped her thinking in the classroom.

Each of these teacher leaders is a whole and happy person. They lead full lives and have numerous interests outside the classroom. Their balance as people allows them to come to the job each day with a good attitude and that makes them fun to work with.

How might your school be impacted if more teacher leaders focused on the present instead of being wrapped up in the past or a future that will undoubtedly look different? How many of your colleagues are so out of balance in their lives that they find little joy in their work? Could a Present Balance Keeper make a difference in your school?

CONCLUSIONS

Many of you reading this book may say to yourselves that the idea of becoming a Present Balance Keeper makes a lot of sense, but it appears to be a difficult job. You are probably wondering how you can make time to invest in yourself and pursue interests you have set aside while still growing as a teacher. The best way forward is to recognize that evolving into a Present Balance Keeper takes time and may take a number of growth steps before you feel you have dramatically improved your life balance.

There are a number of teachers out there who seem to keep everything in balance. While it may seem intuitive, they are often extremely focused on the choices they make and how their energies are expended to maintain momentum. Being clear about annual goals and priorities is certainly a start. Maintaining an active list of focal points or key personal and professional pursuits allows the Present Balance Keeper to keep an eye on those issues they hope to address.

Finally, to develop as a Present Balance Keeper, you might work to become increasingly strategic in your use of time. By breaking down your daily, weekly, and monthly allocations of time with slight adjustments to some of your activities, you may find yourself able to pursue some of those dormant or unchallenged priorities that will make all the difference in developing balance in your life.

We hope no one reading this book has ever looked in the mirror and seen an unbalanced, unhappy teacher who dwells on the past or obsesses on a future they can't control. On the contrary, you probably see yourself as a teacher who has the ability to effortlessly flow from one activity to another, bringing high levels of energy, commitment, and focus to everything you do. You may have found, however, that this isn't as easy as you may have hoped. Perhaps you or your colleagues have recognized some of the frustrations discussed in this chapter and realize that the teacher in the mirror isn't as present, balanced, and focused as he or she could be.

Our personal and professional lives will continue to bring us numerous challenges that we can't possibly anticipate and there will likely be numerous frustrations for us along the way. Even the most well-balanced individual can be thrown off track with just a few unexpected events. Therefore, we encourage the dedication of teacher leaders as Present Balance Keepers, knowing that this dedication will help us be more effective professionals, keep us healthier and happier, and prepare us to serve and support others in capturing the moment and maintaining balance.

For the Present Balance Keeper, we chose this abstract teeter-totter image with a large "P" and "B" within it to remind you to be both present and to maintain balance in your life. We hope that this symbol can remind you how important these two factors are for teacher leadership. By being present, you can take advantage of opportunities to learn and grow in the moment and by staying balanced, you can bring more energy to your work and ensure that your journey is a long, fulfilling one.

9

The Servant

Caring for persons, the more able and the less able serving each other, is the rock upon which a good society is built.

—Robert Greenleaf

The Servant Defined

The Servant is a teacher who leads by supporting and developing others. Servants stay in touch with the needs of their colleagues and support them in their capacity to reflect on their current contributions and future opportunities for growth and improvement. They make outstanding contributions to the school while simultaneously helping everyone around them contribute more. In the classroom, Servants are unmistakably in charge. They demonstrate control by making the service of students their utmost priority. Servants aren't weak or subservient. They are strong enough to consistently demonstrate excellence while creating a sense of connection that helps everyone around them get better at what they do.

Why We Need the Servant

Due to the authoritarian roots of our educational system, the teacher groups we have worked with have seemed uncomfortable when considering teacher leadership in terms of the Servant model. Despite leaders like Mahatma Gandhi, Martin Luther King, Jr., and Mother Teresa, all examples of leaders who provided a transcendent impact by focusing on the needs of others, we still struggle at times, feeling that it is a contradiction to propose that a leader serves. The focus on hierarchy in the past has created an immutable line between boss and worker or between master and servant.

In most professions, the complexity of the work has been elevated to a level where the harsh lines between traditional manager and worker roles fail to enable the kind of flexibility and creativity we need to get the job done. The best organizations have leaders who develop an organic awareness of when it is time to lead, when to allow others to lead, and when to serve and support the overarching system around them.

We understand the importance of this balance in schools and recognize that a leadership style focused on service does not mean submission or servitude. Whether you are a principal or teacher leader, being committed to service is a belief system and a state of mind. Teacher leaders who comprehend the merits of service and adopt a service mentality will reap numerous benefits and will help their schools more effectively embrace a flexible and competitive school culture.

The Servant: Advantages and Benefits

They Maximize Creativity and Innovation by Serving the Learning Needs of Their Colleagues

Servant leadership, at its core, is all about the leaders' desire to explore the gifts of others and facilitate bringing those gifts to the organization (Blanchard, 2009). Organizations that have embraced servant leadership are blessed with leaders who make it their mission to enhance the strengths, contributions, and capacities of others. By investing time, energy, and focus on improving and sustaining others, a culture is developed where learning is enhanced and all members of the group grow and evolve.

Servant leadership is a concept that applies to a number of disciplines. Teacher leaders with a service orientation, however, have a number of unique advantages and opportunities. While in many traditional leadership roles, principals, superintendents, and other managers have a certain degree of hierarchical power, the teacher leader has authority in the school due to their influence and ability to connect with and motivate others. Those teachers who have emerged as teacher leaders may find it easier to establish the authentic relationships with their colleagues that are required to create a rich, learned environment where risks are taken and growth opportunities are seized as they emerge.

A new teacher, for example, will likely be far more willing to discuss in detail the successes and failures of a particular lesson with a thoughtful and influential teacher leader in their school than they would with their principal. This may be due to the fear the new teacher may have of looking weak or uncertain.

Service-oriented teacher leaders can help a school nurture more creative ideas in a safe, yet engaging environment. New ideas will continue to be important moving forward and teacher leaders who can serve the needs of others will help the entire system come up with new innovations for making a difference.

They Continue to Focus on Goals, Not the System

Teacher leaders who embrace a mission in service are invariably in tune with their values and beliefs. While systemic conditions may ebb and flow, values and beliefs that are deeply entrenched and emotionally bound hold firm. Teacher leaders with a service orientation are often able to focus directly on the goals at hand. They are not interrupted by political or systemic conditions that may cause distractions.

If a school invests in a particular curriculum and training program, works diligently at its adoption, implementation, and assessment, then discovers that the program is an abject failure, a teacher leader who is focused on service won't be tempted to stay the course just because of systemic pressures. His or her mission in service will press them to prioritize and attempt to meet the objectives of those higher-ranking values and beliefs.

Scholars of servant leadership as well as thoughtful leader practitioners, who understand what it means to apply this concept to their work, never forget that their most important job is providing valued service to their clients in association with the work that they do (Blanchard, 2009). If the service they provide doesn't differentiate them, they won't be competitive or relevant anymore. By keeping a focus on this service orientation, the distractions of change can be dramatically minimized. This is true in business and industry, as well as schools today.

They Enhance Collaboration and Cooperation in the School and Beyond

One of the most notable aspects of a truly evolved professional is selflessness. Teacher leaders who are Servants are so confident in their own capacities and are so clear about their mission and vision that they can safely focus on others to serve a greater overarching and collective mission.

Those of you who are veteran teachers can probably recall those moments when you were no longer new to the classroom and worried every minute about your performance, and were able instead to shift your focus directly to the learning needs of the students you served. This transition from a focus on ourselves to a focus on those we serve is a microcosm of what teacher leaders do every day.

Thus, teacher leaders as Servants are willing to be there to support colleagues, as well as other professionals they meet around the block or around the world. Almost intuitively, leaders who understand the power of service recognize the magical exchange that occurs when we learn to put the needs of others first—and give. One benefit for the Servant is a network of colleagues, both in the school and beyond, that would undoubtedly be willing to return the favor as needs arise.

They Promote Individual and Team Support During Difficult and Toxic Times

Even the best schools run into difficult challenges. Teachers may betray one another. Unsettling problems may arise at the superintendent or board level. The students and the community may disappoint the teachers on staff and an overarching sense of toxicity in the organization may emerge.

For years, practitioners and scholars have studied this notion of a temporary or long-term toxic organizational climate. What many scholars have come to believe is that one of the quickest ways to turn a toxic environment around or respond to those unhealthy seasons of toxicity is to establish and maintain a dedication to a service mentality (Greenleaf, 1970).

Schools that have teacher leaders who understand what it means to be the Servant can respond more thoughtfully during these toxic times. They can forgive, offer support, and keep bigger goals and objectives in mind without obsessing about egos, positions, or power. If feelings have been hurt, friendships betrayed, or performance fallen short of expectation, these teacher leaders have enough confidence in themselves, their profession, and their schools to refrain from making these disappointments personal. They fall back on the service mentality, which puts the focus on serving the needs of others.

Looking in the Mirror: Becoming the Servant

Once again, consider your existing mental models as they relate to the teacher leader as Servant. Rating your positions on this scale will provide you an honest look at yourself in relation to this type of teacher leadership.

Classroom Applications for the Servant

Old Reflection		*New Reflection*
By working together, we become more efficient classroom managers.	5 4 3 2 1 0 1 2 3 4 5 ⟷	By collaborating, we clarify our mission in service and help develop each other's strengths and improve our individual and collective capacities.
Rules and policies are important. They help to ensure control and consistency.	5 4 3 2 1 0 1 2 3 4 5 ⟷	Rules and policies are important. They help to create an environment that improves my service.
I expect my students to come to me. When they arrive, I will help them learn.	5 4 3 2 1 0 1 2 3 4 5 ⟷	I go to my students. I seek out their strengths and help to serve their learning needs in the time we have together.

Discussion of Classroom Applications

The old analogy of the teacher being the fountain of knowledge is long outdated. Even the best and brightest teachers cannot provide information to students as quickly as technology can. Teachers, however, are more important than ever in that they help students define their filters and they support students in their capacity to look within themselves, find their strengths, and apply lessons learned in school to their real lives in a meaningful way.

This personalized and differentiated mission in learning is what we have come to expect in school today. The more intimate mission cannot be accomplished, however, if teachers continue to see themselves as the fountains of knowledge where students gather eagerly at their feet to learn.

Schoolwide Change for the Servant

Old Reflection		*New Reflection*
I am a proud professional. I do not serve anyone.	5 4 3 2 1 0 1 2 3 4 5 ◄──►	I am a proud professional. Serving my students and my colleagues is a privilege and a calling.
I am here to deliver the curriculum. I will try to lead as many students as possible to the water, but I can't make them drink.	5 4 3 2 1 0 1 2 3 4 5 ◄──►	I am here to serve the learning needs of my students. The curriculum is available to me to support my mission of service.
I wait to hear the principal's vision for the school.	5 4 3 2 1 0 1 2 3 4 5 ◄──►	I expect to follow the school's vision.
My mission in serving my students is the most important work being done in the school.	5 4 3 2 1 0 1 2 3 4 5 ◄──►	My principal and others certainly can influence my never-ending pursuit. Fundamentally, my job in the classroom is clear.

Indeed, no one said being the Servant was easy. It is common for teachers to take things personally in the classroom or fall into teacher-centered practice, which completely turns the service orientation upside-down. However, teachers who have come to understand a service-oriented practice enjoy meaningful relationships with their students and create classroom cultures that are authentic and safe.

Being connected to students in this more focused and intimate way takes a great deal more energy and understanding than teaching to the masses and hoping they get what we teach. But the learning of our students is the reason most of us embarked on this trip. The road may be more difficult, but the journey and the destination are much preferred.

Discussion of Schoolwide Change

The Servant clearly understands that the mission is service. The higher aspirations of meeting the learning needs of students are of utmost importance. While changes to the curriculum, new materials, new schedules, and new state and federal mandates will continue, the Servant is wise enough to hover above the fray. He or she remembers that the mission is a profound one that revolves around service to mankind and the ultimate journey toward self-actualization. Principals, politicians, adamant colleagues, and the flavor-of-the-month in school reform will come and go, but Servants know why they come to work each day.

Emerging teacher leaders must keep in mind that the concept of service for teachers represents an orientation to the work rather than a descriptor of how the work is executed. Doctors and judges are on a mission of service in their communities. A doctor serves the health and well-being of patients while the judge serves the law of the land. Teacher leaders are likewise on an important mission of service and their ability to comprehend what this mission means helps to drive their progress and capacities. To better understand this concept, consider the details below.

STRATEGIES FOR BECOMING AND SUPPORTING THE SERVANT

The evolution of the Servant as an aspect of teacher leadership is made difficult by conventions and perspectives from the past. Emergence of the Servant can be enhanced by specific actions of teacher leaders. Listed below are some of the steps teachers can take to begin their personal evolution as a teacher leader and to stimulate this type of leadership in their schools.

Single-Student Impacts Strategy

We live in an era of what is called school accountability and we use data points when describing students. We talk about relative relationship to standard, cohort group comparisons, and even look at demographics as a means for making improvements to the instructional program. While these discussions are essential, it has been our experience that the most effective schools are able to use large cohort data points while simultaneously focusing at the granular level to consider the individual needs of the students they serve.

We tend to look at the students we serve first as part of a school and then as members of a class. This perspective dates back to the paradigms set in the early twentieth century. Our economy was based on the capacity of faceless groups to move together and perform tasks as directed.

When changing this paradigm, the Servant knows the pyramid must be flipped upside down. Individual needs of students must come first. Their learning, growth, and developmental needs should be considered in relationship to the class, then the school as a whole.

While this may seem like a good theoretical discussion, changing the paradigm in actuality involves consistent and deliberate action. Teacher leaders must put forth the notion that their mission in service is, first and foremost, the individual learning needs of each student. And they must keep this goal in sight during the school improvement process. It is so easy to get embroiled in political battles and pedestrian turf wars that may seem important at the moment. Perhaps this is why so many successful teacher leaders keep pictures of their students nearby. Glancing into the eyes of the students they serve helps them keep the needs of individuals at the fore.

To bring this strategy to fruition, teacher leaders can put single-student impacts on the agenda when considering a change at department, grade level, or school improvement team meetings. Business as usual would have the team address how a proposed changed would affect the school in aggregate or reshape a particular group of students. In a single-student impacts discussion, however, the team considers the impact on individual students. How will this impact Francis or Cheryl from third hour?

When you personalize the discussion and direct the thinking to individual students, it is likely that conversations about potential changes will take on a more serious tenor and the energy level in a room can change. Debating abstract data swings is never as emotionally engaging as thinking about individual students. The Servant understands that they are not there to move the bell curve. It is their mission to impact the lives of people.

Sacred Exchange Strategy

Servants focus on the learning needs of each student, but they don't think about it in the abstract. The culmination of their efforts as teachers comes at that sacred moment when students "see it" and learn something new. Ultimately, to serve, support, and enhance the sacred exchange is all teachers want to do.

To apply this strategy, teacher leaders can infuse questions into the school improvement process related to "sacred exchange impacts." For example, in a team meeting about a change for next year, a teacher leader focused on serving the needs of individuals should ask, "How does this impact the sacred exchange between teacher and student at the point of learning?"

While not every discussion revolves around the sacred exchange, it is clear that the best schools leading the most significant levels of change keep that exchange at the forefront of their planning efforts. The degree to which that exchange is valued, discussed, improved upon, and held as "sacred" will drive to a great extent the depth of change possible in the school.

Public Declaration of Service Strategy

Servant leaders tend to toil away in quiet, subtle ways. Their support of their colleagues at work may come in short bursts, driven by quiet conversations held extemporaneously as the need arises. As a result, a Public Declaration of Service might not seem natural, even to the Servant teacher leader.

Nonetheless, making the service orientation a publically stated priority is important. This strategy involves a public declaration that service is a key component of the work being done at the school. The declaration of service should be clear that the mandate extends to students, parents, and the community that supports the school.

Keep in mind that the notion that schools exist as vessels of service isn't necessarily a mental model that will sit well in the hearts and minds of all community members. Many of them came from traditional K–12 backgrounds where, unfortunately, the priorities of these older institutions may have revolved around outdated images of authority and control.

To make this public declaration of service more effective, we recommend that teachers take every chance to communicate that it is their mission to serve the learning needs of their students. This priority should be emphasized in open houses and other public events. When dealing with parents, veteran teachers can certainly attest to how powerful it is to tell parents that you are there to support and serve. When schools commit to responsive service, the community and parents are more likely to support that effort and become more cooperative partners in the mission of the school.

When you implement this strategy, it is helpful for interested teacher leaders to take time throughout the year to evaluate how well they are spreading their message of service. Are we communicating with parents in a way that shows we are there to serve them? Do our students know? What steps can we take to bring more clarity about this effort to the students and their parents?

School Improvement as Service Strategy

Some of the most effective schools set academic goals that revolve around specific assessment results. They may, for example, determine that a 5 percent to 7 percent improvement in state math scores for a certain cohort group is well within their reach for a particular academic year. They may determine that a reduction in absenteeism or dropout rates is a motivating outcome. Thoughtful school leaders understand that these academic and effective benchmarks serve as important but not necessarily all-encompassing signals of what could become a transformational journey in service.

While ensuring these deeper connections to the school's values and beliefs, it is helpful to revisit and reflect as a staff that learning is the ultimate goal and that the efforts of the group should serve the learning objectives of the students. Engaging in these discussions about service and making a heartfelt collegial commitment to these generational, big-picture pursuits, it is likely that those involved will become emotionally engaged in the work at hand.

This step in the change process is not about motivation, it is about clarification. Teacher leaders need to clarify their big-picture service orientation for the shorter-term efforts in test scores and training to make sense in the bigger context.

Are you in touch with your own mission in service? Do you know the big-picture pursuits you are after? Most likely you did not enter the profession to ensure a 5% improvement in middle school science scores. While that might be the result of your actions, reminding yourself of your heartfelt aspirations will always drive you to work harder.

Schoolwide Service Projects Strategy

Service learning has a place in many schools today. While it exists in many P–12 settings, it also carries over to a number of colleges and universities throughout the world. One of the reasons schools have always been at the center of outreach efforts in local, national, and international service projects is that teachers and fellow school leaders tend to have a service orientation.

The propensity to support service learning is there at the onset. There is no substitute for taking substantive action as a mechanism for supporting what is an emergent but heartfelt sensibility. Schools that consistently participate in some type of service project or charitable work understand the value of service and how it can inform and support those being served and those engaged in the process of helping out.

Several years ago, some highly impoverished southern Arizona schools decided to begin a number of long-term service projects with schools just over the Mexican border. While these poorly funded, rural Arizona schools certainly lacked many of the accoutrements of their well-funded neighbors to the north, they reached out with great pride in helping their less-fortunate neighbors to the south. What these school leaders discovered was that by accepting their own conditions and deciding to serve others, the students and teachers alike developed a greater appreciation for what they had rather than a focus on what they lacked. That sense of empowerment and control led to improved test scores and a better overall school climate.

Transcendent Teacher Leaders in Action: The Servant

Each of the teacher leaders profiled in this book exemplifies what it means to be a service-oriented teacher leader. Kate was dedicated to serving the low-performing students in her school whose backgrounds and profiles didn't "fit" what was typical. Khris served both her students as well as an entire population of children in a town in Afghanistan. Mary Ann saw the development of her talent as a mechanism for working toward the betterment of her students and her community.

As a coach, Jim broke the mold in many ways. Many football coaches expect a service orientation; however, they seem to think that they are the ones to be served. We have observed a number of coaches who treat their players like privates in boot camp, breaking them down at every turn and making participation on the team the loftiest of aspirations that isn't open to everyone.

Jim had a different mentality. Years before, he had read several books by Dr. Ken Blanchard, the author of *The One Minute Manager* (1983). Blanchard, one of the seminal authors in servant leadership, has consistently espoused the importance of reaching out, serving others, and making those who work for you feel important and appreciated.

When Jim became the head football coach, he encouraged students to try out. He went out of his way to support kids who might have had a tough time coming to practice or had struggles at home. While he had high expectations for his players, Jim never forgot this service modality and supported his players at every turn. Just as Dr. Blanchard would have predicted, Jim's players rewarded his dedication with loyalty and a desire to work with an enthusiasm that's unmatched.

How different would your school be if it embraced what it means to be a servant leader? How would the students and community respond to a culture and climate immersed in this sensibility? Undoubtedly there are teacher leaders in your school who are already making service a big part of their mission and work. What would the addition of more service-oriented teacher leaders mean to your progress in continuous improvement?

CONCLUSIONS

The Servant is an aspect of teacher leadership easily lost in generalities and good intentions. This is why we have attempted to be as specific as possible about the steps teacher leaders can take in service that not only improve the climate of the school, but also reinforce the position and authority teachers have in the school.

When a layperson hears the term "teacher leader as Servant," they may mistakenly assume that the profession has been downgraded. In this context, however, service-oriented teacher leaders stimulate the deepest levels of improvement and can take the position of teacher to exalted levels.

As a brand new teacher looking into the mirror, you might have felt concern about your ability to exert authority. Was the idea of seeing yourself as a servant intimidating, causing you to feel weak or unprofessional? We hope that a closer examination of yourself and the profession will help you realize the true power and influence that comes along with those leaders who are brave enough to serve. Are you ready to be a teacher who leads through service?

For the Servant, we have chosen the image of a hand reaching gently forward. Teacher leaders operating as Servants understand that the act of reaching out to others is done in a quiet way, but has a huge impact. Given the chaos, confusion, and frustration that can dominate the culture in schools, we hope this image can be a reminder of what's possible for teacher leaders who keep a service orientation at the forefront and reach out to others to make a difference.

10

The Inquisitor

I have no particular talent. I am merely inquisitive.

—Albert Einstein

THE INQUISITOR DEFINED

Inquisitors are teacher leaders who inspire their students, their colleagues, and themselves with thoughtful, strategic, purposeful, and emotionally bound questions. They know that life's journey is based on the pursuit of seminal questions. Our brains are coaxed into increased levels of engagement, depending on the quality of the questions we ask and answer. Individuals and teams alike can dramatically change their journey in teaching when they are thoughtful about the answers they seek. The Inquisitor helps find the best answers by pursuing and asking the best questions.

WHY WE NEED THE INQUISITOR

Successful schools where teacher leadership drives significant levels of change do not pursue unproductive questions like, "What's wrong with these students? What's wrong with the parents? Why is the government ruining our profession?" (Reason, 2010). While all of us have probably asked ourselves these questions in moments of fatigue and frustration, the school can't get very far by expending energies on these toxic pursuits. They may provide a brief catharsis, but focusing on them leads nowhere. After all, what's more stressful than being introduced to a problem and then learning there is little you can do about it?

When we are more thoughtful about our questions, we can be more purposeful and productive in our journey. The Inquisitor understands this exchange and inspires others by thoughtfully engaging them with provocative questions. He or she is willing to rigorously engage in the pursuit of answers. In an era in which we face many difficult questions, the teacher leader as Inquisitor helps us identify the questions that matter and then focuses and reframes our responses.

The Inquisitor: Advantages and Benefits

They Promote Greater Levels of Team Unity and Connectedness

Think about your happiest and highest-functioning experience as a team member. There was probably an emotional bond holding the team together that brought unity to your efforts en route to a particular goal. This kind of team does remarkable work. What makes the difference is its level of engagement and connectedness. Every school has teams of teachers who are capable of transcendent outcomes if only they would work together in an empowered and connected way.

The teacher leader as Inquisitor can inspire emotional connection with his or her skill at asking and answering important questions. When teams work together and use inquiry in their collaboration, they learn to challenge each other on a consistent basis. Trust is established and they feel comfortable in strengthening their inquiry levels. They push each other to their limits. Such an emotional bond can build team confidence, leading them to ask, "Why can't we do more? What can we do to break through to the next level of performance?"

Working together inspires deeper levels of neurological engagement (Achterman & Loertscher, 2008). We are a species that operates more effectively together than we do on our own. Our most successful ancestors were those who could work with another group as a means of survival (Johnson, 2003). You could even make the case that we are naturally wired to work in teams. When asking questions together, we can seek the best possible answers.

They Break Down Barriers and Negate Groupthink

The Inquisitor can help well-intentioned groups overcome limitations of their thinking. They ask questions that challenge outdated paradigms. Inquisitors in schools with high dropout rates may ask a team, "Does the fact that we suspend students for being tardy lead to higher failure rates? Are there other actions we could take to respond to tardiness that would solve the problem without creating failure in other areas?"

To the layperson, it might seem obvious that policies like suspending students for being tardy are counterintuitive, but through the years we have witnessed these discussions in schools. We have come to associate certain systemic responses with certain student behaviors. The Inquisitor's mind is agile enough to move outside of these paradigms to ask questions hoping to shape new and improved outcomes.

We still function under the onus of paradigms that existed long before anyone reading this book began a career in teaching. Our difficulty with identifying novel alternative perspectives is also due to what sociologists call groupthink. Groupthink occurs when our familiarity with one another causes us to bring our thoughts, ideas, habits, and beliefs into alignment to such a degree that we begin to lack the diversity of perspective that might otherwise enrich our work together (Janis, 1982).

It is the role of Inquisitors to break the debilitating impact of groupthink. In this way, Inquisitors are fire starters. But they don't start the fire and run away. Instead, they ask provocative questions and stick around to articulate the most thoughtful of answers.

They Inspire Research

By establishing a school culture where rigorous and relevant questions are consistently asked and answered, the Inquisitor is also likely to create an environment where greater attention to research emerges. Asking a question like, "How can we help our middle-level, English as a Second Language students improve in the language portion of the state proficiency test?" may inspire research into where students are falling behind and what interventions other schools are using in a similar circumstance.

If you don't ask a specific question, you won't get a specific answer. So, questions like, "What's wrong with the parents of this community?" or "Why don't people appreciate teachers more?" are not the kinds of questions that lend themselves to research and the Inquisitor does not waste time on them.

Inquisitors may, on the other hand, ask question about students' previous classes, types of interventions recommended, or the systemic process of transitioning from one class to the next. Each question would spark a different analysis, both in the data sets and in the processes the organization uses. When asking thought-provoking questions, the team may pursue a new hypothesis that requires research initiatives that may be used again and again.

They Generate Deep Levels of Innovation and Creativity

Asking thought-provoking questions helps a team evaluate new possibilities and allows them to be more creative. It's easy to get caught up in day-to-day tasks, such as answering e-mail or scheduling meetings. But the questions from Inquisitors encourage us to look beyond immediate demands and to think deeper about change outcomes that would help improve the school climate.

Classroom Applications for the Inquisitor

Old Reflection		*New Reflection*
The work of the class is organized around the agreed upon curriculum and/or text.	5 4 3 2 1 0 1 2 3 4 5 ◄──►	The work of the class is organized around big-picture essential questions based on the curriculum.
In class, teachers have the answers.	5 4 3 2 1 0 1 2 3 4 5 ◄──►	In class, teachers have the questions. The answers are everywhere.
The teachers check the students to see if they have the "right" answers.	5 4 3 2 1 0 1 2 3 4 5 ◄──►	Students review the questions, propose answers, and then collectively evaluate.

LOOKING IN THE MIRROR: BECOMING THE INQUISITOR

Just as we asked of you in each of the chapters in this book, consider your existing mental models as they relate to the teacher leader as Inquisitor. Try to evaluate your teaching practice according to this scale quickly without analyzing it too deeply. This will provide you an honest look at yourself in relation to this type of teacher leadership.

Discussion of Classroom Applications

There are two major advantages to using big-picture questions to deliver the curriculum. First, asking big-picture questions about content can spark student interest. It helps students understand why the learning is important in the first place. Second, when forces in- or outside the school drive changes in the curriculum, it likely will have little effect on big-picture pursuits that students are investigating. Even if a major change happens involving textbooks, the curriculum, or the state test, the overarching questions that drive the

Schoolwide Change for the Inquisitor

Old Reflection		*New Reflection*
We question the things that keep us from doing the impossible.	5 4 3 2 1 0 1 2 3 4 5 ◄──►	We question what is possible.
We constantly question the system and the people in it.	5 4 3 2 1 0 1 2 3 4 5 ◄──►	We question ourselves and our ability to impact the system.
Questions are used for procrastination.	5 4 3 2 1 0 1 2 3 4 5 ◄──►	Questions are used for learning stimulation.

need for the course and spark the desire to pursue the subject will continue to shape the efforts of the teacher leader.

The notion of the teacher as Inquisitor is also a valuable model given the continued challenges teachers face in attempting to keep up with a world that is changing so rapidly. In an information age, classrooms cannot be dependent on teachers having all the answers. Instead, the best classrooms now and in the future will take advantage of spontaneous and continuous learning opportunities stimulated by students pursuing a carefully crafted set of inquiries narrowed and defined by clarifying questions provided by the teachers who guide them. Teachers then become the facilitators of the pursuit of answers, rather than the proverbial fountains of knowledge themselves.

Discussion of Schoolwide Change

Schools today certainly face a number of tough questions. Legislators, the community, and a more demanding student body will continue to question the system of public education and push it to its limits. In the past, teachers and principals have often found themselves questioning the system and perhaps felt like throwing their hands in the air as they awaited the answer to what might be a very difficult or somewhat imponderable question regarding their work.

Teacher leaders working as Inquisitors continue to ask tough questions of their profession, their school, and themselves. The difference is that they see themselves being the very system they are inquiring about. As they wonder aloud about the capacities of the system, they are quick to acknowledge that those capacities will evolve in direct proportion to their ability to ask and answer the tough questions ahead.

In the past, those interested in blocking change efforts would use questions to filibuster the change conversation and to keep meaningful change from happening. The Inquisitor, however, won't let this happen and instead won't ask the question unless he or she is committed to pursuing the answer in the system and within themselves.

Strategies for Becoming and Supporting the Inquisitor

A fundamental reason why an inquiry-based approach is beneficial is that the learning process is greatly stimulated by asking thoughtful questions (Coulter, 2006). This is true for learners at all levels. If more Inquisitors emerge in schools, the learning culture can become more engaged, focused, and driven toward better and more specific outcomes. What follows are actions that teacher leaders can take to become Inquisitors and to support this approach to teacher leadership.

Raise-the-Bar Questioning Strategy

The teacher leader as Inquisitor is always contemplating, "How high is high?" in relation to his or her own talents and abilities. While the profession may have established certain conventions about how much a teacher can do and the degree to which they can create change, the Inquisitor is willing to play the role of paradigm buster and openly inquire as to how much more is possible if there is a collective will to go beyond old paradigms or limits.

A powerful yet controversial example of this notion of raising the bar by asking a previously unattainable question came along in the early 2000s when No Child Left Behind (NCLB) was voted into law. According to NCLB, every student in every school in the United States would be performing at standard by 2015. That goal forced every school to ask if it was possible to reach every child and ensure that they were in fact performing at sufficient levels in each of the core content areas.

We found ourselves at times bogged down with discussions about the merits of the assessments, funding challenges, and various punitive measures that were taken state-by-state as a result of the failure to meet adequate yearly progress. This goal has forced schools to ask questions about their performance that perhaps they hadn't considered before. Unfortunately for many schools, it was a paradigm-breaking moment for the school to openly question whether they could reach every student and help them perform to standard.

NCLB represented a change force that came from the outside and pushed its way into our schools. Other examples of raising the bar, however, have come from within, when teacher leaders openly ask bar-raising questions about what's possible.

Everyone in the community would have supported Jim's effort as a football coach if it had been the goal of his program to be competitive at a local level. Instead, he openly asked what would happen if the program challenged itself to be competitive at the state level. Khris could have had a powerful influence on the students in Afghanistan simply by raising some money and supporting the intervention efforts of others. Instead, she asked a bar-raising question and received a transformational response. Teacher leaders who ask bar-raising questions stir us emotionally and can have a profound impact on the schools they serve.

Unpopular Questions Strategy

Yet another gift of the Inquisitor is a willingness to ask the unspoken or unpopular question. This is done to push the group to move beyond its comfort level to find novel solutions for the team's challenges. "Why are our African American and Latino students being suspended at twice the rate of our white students? Is this a reflection of something in our system that could be changed?"

Asking these types of questions requires a degree of comfort within the group and confidence in one another. If these tough questions are never posed, it is likely that difficult challenges will go unanswered in the organization. The Inquisitor is there to ensure that the next generation does not emerge without that question being addressed.

The Inquisitor must be careful in posing these types of questions to avoid coming off as accusatory. Unpopular questions are best asked in a private environment where teachers and staff members can reflect on their concerns about the school. This doesn't mean that these questions and the pursuit of their answers can't also be taken public and openly acknowledged. In fact, this is an important step.

Schools that have made the greatest progress in leading change are those that have been brave enough to bring difficult, uncomfortable, and hard-to-answer questions to the forefront of their pursuits. Teacher leadership takes courage and this is an example wherein the teacher leader as Inquisitor must be brave enough to ask a tough question and pursue what might be an important answer.

The habit of asking this type of question can emerge organically with a teacher leader who is aware of how important it is to an institution. They can also be strategically baked into particular points of process in which teams may ask, "What are the hard questions we should be asking ourselves right now?" or "Are there hard questions that we are avoiding?"

Minimally, these gut-check moments will give everyone a chance to reflect and be honest with one another. While revealing problems and challenges, these moments of honesty also bring the team closer together.

Empowered Questions Strategy

Inquisitors tend to put their focus on the pursuit of questions that they are empowered within their school to answer. While they may engage at times in the cathartic inquiry as to how to overcome school funding issues or problems with the state legislature or board of education, they do not allow these questions to become the focus of their professional efforts.

They recognize instead that they are empowered to pursue important questions about student achievement, behavior, and the potential outcome of their local school improvement efforts. Inquisitors, therefore, are disciplined in their inquiry efforts and will ask with greater interest those questions over which they have most control in finding the answers.

Wide and Narrow Questions Strategy

Teacher leaders understand the power of inquiry and know that there is a time and place for specific and focused questions, as well as for open-ended and creative questions. "How can we reach students in a more profound way?" or "How can we come together as a staff and stay connected and supportive of one another?" are broad questions that will arguably never be completely answered. They do, however, serve two important functions.

First, they help to stimulate creativity without narrowing the focus and, second, they help to define the learning culture. In looking at issues related to students, for example, asking "How can we help students feel calm, connected, and focused at school?" is a much broader, open-ended question than, "How can we change our demerit policy?"

A penalty system may be a specific response that may need to be evaluated, but the former question may get teachers thinking creatively about solutions. Creating a rich, focused, and inviting school climate might dramatically reduce the suspension rate in a school and the number of options for creating that type of environment are unlimited.

There are times when more specific questions are essential and the teacher leader as Inquisitor knows when to make that shift. If a team of eighth-grade teachers realizes that their state math scores are suffering and the transition to ninth grade is not working for their students, they would be well served to ask, "How can we improve our transitions for pre-algebra students to the integrated algebra program while simultaneously preparing them for their state math test their sophomore year?"

Note the specificity of the challenge and the recognition of the issues of transitions, curriculum alignment, instruction, and intervention to ensure that students are ready. That level of specificity is much better than asking, "Why can't these kids pass the tenth-grade math test?" or "What's wrong with the middle school math teachers? Why can't they send us kids ready to learn?" These broad, open-ended questions keep us from getting at the heart of the problem.

Inspirational Questions Strategy

When exploring the Inquisitor's role, we have seen how the power of inquiry can pull team members together and get them thinking collectively about school challenges. Teacher leaders as Inquisitors also ask questions to provide inspiration.

At a salient moment, a strong teacher may ask his or her colleagues, "What kind of school do we want our students to experience?" or "Does anyone here think that we are doing all that we can for these kids? Does anyone think that by working together more thoughtfully we can reach more students and make this school a better place for all of us to work?"

Using a well positioned, inspiring question can shift the focus and energy of a team and can ignite better planning and execution as a result. These heartfelt questions can help inspire all of us to both dream and take action in thoughtful and profound ways.

Critical Questions Strategy

Many schools instituting professional learning communities also establish a series of critical and strategic questions designed to inspire the deepest levels of school change. These questions have helped inspire a number of useful discussions about school improvement and serve to avoid what DuFour et al. (2008) referred to as "blaboration" (instead of collaboration). Questions, therefore, are an important part of what it means to build a collaborative community of learners.

Even if your school does not have professional learning communities, it is important to use critical questions as the basis of school improvement planning, professional development, and any opportunities teachers have to work together. Questions stimulate creativity and solutions.

Process Point Questions Strategy

Leaders at all levels need to use questions more strategically when doing the following:

1. Running meetings: Some teams begin each meeting by asking questions about the purpose of the meeting and what the team hopes to achieve. From a management perspective, this helps make good use of time. From a leadership perspective, this merges into the next step, identifying the overarching questions.

   If, for example, the purpose of the meeting is how to improve middle school initiatives in science, that would be the narrow focus. The big-picture questions would be how to get middle school students to love science and to excel at the highest levels when they move on to high school. Even if the agenda is rather benign, awareness of the overarching questions help improve levels of engagement and focus.

2. Conducting school improvement goal-setting sessions: Over the years, the school improvement process has changed dramatically. A generation ago, it was quite popular to have large and unwieldy strategic plans. Today, the school improvement planning process is less cumbersome and more action oriented (Martin, McCrone, Bower, & Dindyal, 2005; O'Reilly & Frank, 2006). When setting building- and district-level school

improvement goals, it is helpful to discuss annual, quarterly, monthly, or weekly goals with a specific question that will ignite the pursuit.

If a building has a goal of helping every third- and fourth-grade student reach state standards in math, the third- and fourth-grade elementary team may consider the following questions:

a. How can we offer a third- and fourth-grade math curriculum that challenges the students who are already at or beyond standard?

b. How can we support students who are close to meeting state standards? What additional supports do they need?

c. What type of differentiation do we need to provide students who are struggling dramatically to meet standards?

d. What special population considerations do we need to consider in meeting standards? Are there certain populations currently performing lower than others? What is the cause of this challenge? What can we do to specifically support these students?

In thinking about each of the questions above, imagine it is third- and fourth-grade teachers who are leading the inquiry. Rather than wait for the principal or curriculum director to identify strategies and process considerations, imagine how powerful the conversation could become if the teacher leaders themselves asked these questions and pursued the answers. There is a greater sense of ownership and engagement when we know the questions we're posing are our responsibility to answer.

Question Criteria Strategy

Teacher leaders who want to be Inquisitors need to be astute at distinguishing good questions from bad questions.

Below find five questions that teacher leaders can ask to clarify the inquiry pursuit.

FIVE QUESTIONS ABOUT INQUIRY

1. Is the question answerable?
2. Do we own this question?
3. Are we empowered to have an impact on the result?
4. Is this problem sufficiently challenging?
5. Is this question worth our pursuit?

The first question is important because we often get bogged down with questions like "What's wrong with our students?" We could spend a lifetime identifying the maladies of students, teachers, principals, parents, and the profession as a whole. Ensuring this specificity prevents teams from careening off and wasting time.

The second question related to ownership can certainly result in interesting discussions. When asking this question of a group, there will be those who consistently argue that the heavy hand of the government, central office, or building-level administration somehow keeps a particular question from being owned by the local teacher group. In many cases, however, there is a greater degree of ownership in terms of practical application than they might assume. Ultimately, by asking the ownership question, we introduce the possibility that at least a portion of the problem can or should be owned at the local teacher level.

The third question on empowerment is connected to the second question. Be specific about empowerment. Teacher leaders can be clear about the change process in their school and how the school may have empowered them to pursue the issue. A team of teachers that begins to check alterations to the bus schedule, for example, may discover that even the most empowerment-oriented administrators are unwilling to relinquish decisions about transportation.

The fourth question, deciding if a question is sufficiently challenging, is designed to clarify and inspire. In some cases, groups are limited to seeking goals that are not commensurate with the team's real capabilities. They do not inspire creativity or imagination. Pushing for a 2% growth rate may not represent the true capabilities of a bright, thoughtful, and engaged team. Setting the bar high enough makes a difference.

The last question should not be answered too quickly. Many times, educators take on too many projects. This is an excellent time for the Inquisitor and the team to thoroughly probe a question and evaluate it against other pursuits and priorities. Asking this last question may result in a team finding that their pursuit is noble, well-intentioned, interesting, and potentially worthwhile. If the sacrifice of time and engagement does not make the pursuit of the question worth the effort, however, other questions may be the priority.

Transcendent Teacher Leaders in Action: The Inquisitor

The transcendent teacher leaders featured in this book were each empowered by a difficult set of questions. Kate could have wondered, "What's wrong with these kids? Why won't they listen when they're given a chance?" Instead she asked, "How can I reach them? How can I serve their learning needs in what must be a very difficult circumstance?"

Khris also asked some unique questions. She could have wondered how to tell her students about what it means to serve. Instead, she decided to show them. This slight shift in focus led to a dramatically different set of outcomes.

The questions don't always have to be perfect or even terribly complex. Jim would celebrate a success with his team and ask them, "Can you do even more?" With emotions running high after a win, their collective brain would come alive and begin to grapple with a new standard for success.

Mary Ann didn't just ask, "How can I get these students to pass the test?" Instead, she asked, "How can I teach them to love math and excel?" Each of these teacher leaders asked hard questions. Those hard questions led to more profound pursuits and better answers.

We challenge you to think about the questions you ask and answer each day. If you were thoughtful about the questions in your head and the actions that would result, would they take you in the direction you intend? Looking more broadly at your school, what questions are being pursued by your department or grade level? What about your school improvement team? How much more productive could you be as a teacher leader if you were more purposeful about the questions you sought answers for each day on the job?

Could your school improvement team make a small shift in the questions they ask and get dramatically different results? Could you begin to ask, "How can we reinforce learning beyond the school day?" instead of, "Why won't kids do their homework?" This type of inquiry pursuit can clearly shape the learning trajectory and stimulate deeper levels of engagement (Reason, 2010).

Conclusions

Inquisitors can inspire themselves and their colleagues in many ways. Their ability to establish a culture of inquiry and to purposefully ask better questions can bring the focus and specificity needed to help the school move forward. As you looked into the mirror and visualized your role as a teacher early in your career, you might have worried about the possibility that students would have questions for you that you couldn't answer. Perhaps you saw yourself evolving in the profession and having the answers when the questions came.

This new image of teacher leader as Inquisitor puts us in the position of posing questions and then collaborating with others in the pursuit of answers. The image of the ivory tower professor regaling us with his or her knowledge from on high is far removed from the image of teacher leadership we've illustrated here. We hope you are purposeful in your pursuits as a teacher and become an ongoing promoter of leading the team with thoughtful levels of inquiry.

? The Inquisitor

For the Inquisitor, we chose a simple question mark as a reminder of the importance of questions. We hope that as you see this image, you are reminded how important it is to ask good questions of yourself, of others, and of your institution. We also hope that you mentally associate this simple punctuation mark with the professional pursuits you consider each day.

11

The Detective

Education is not the filling of a pail but the lighting of a fire.
—William Butler Yeats

The Detective Defined

Teacher leaders as Detectives solve mysteries and notice things that the untrained eye can't see. These sleuths spot untapped creativity and potential in their students and colleagues and help bring forth and nurture those hidden talents. Detectives unearth learning challenges in the classroom and identify pathways to resolve those issues for the students they serve. When facing a difficult team challenge, the Detective has the ability to identify the individual and collective skills of the team and those teammates most likely to lend a hand in resolving the problem. In the face of failure and disappointment, the teacher leader as Detective identifies a glimmer of hope and a way to advance and prevail. These leaders don't simply offer blind optimism. Instead, they move through the school with the confidence that they can solve the complex mystery at hand.

Why We Need the Detective

We chose the image of the Detective for this type of teacher leader because both you and we know what detectives do. They seek the truth, look for clues, and notice details and nuances that the layperson often ignores. If they need information, they know how to draw it out. Amidst chaos, the detective can extract meaning and solve a difficult case.

Through the years, we have known teacher leaders who possessed this capacity to discover what is unseen to others. They have the ability to put the pieces together in a unique way—whether it is diagnosing learning problems or seeing gifts and abilities in others that have gone unnoticed. The Detective is the teacher leader who breathes life into the school and closes cases left unsolved for years. In these complex times, teachers who work as Detectives are more important than ever.

The Detective: Advantages and Benefits

They Identify Learning Challenges and Gifts in the Students They Serve

The Detective understands the teaching profession has become highly specialized and specific. They know that studying students carefully will reveal the learning challenges they face as well as opportunities to overcome those challenges.

The Detective is the teacher known throughout the school as having the capacity to work with students with difficult learning challenges, to quickly diagnose their issues and identify mechanisms to support their needs. Like most good detectives in books or movies, teacher leaders as Detectives work best when they have trusted partners with whom to collaborate. Detectives constantly share notes with colleagues and expand their capacity to understand the learning needs of their students.

They Identify and Support Important Leadership Traits in Colleagues

To enable deep levels of school improvement to emerge, the Detective understands that leadership is required from all corners of the organization. These forward-thinking leaders are always looking for leadership capacity in their colleagues. Teachers with special abilities may be called upon by the Detective to step forward and bring their skills to bear on a current challenge. A quiet colleague, who for years made his or her way by obediently following others, may have some unique abilities to take the lead. The Detective is the one who identifies and encourages the exploration of these gifts.

They Identify and Support Important Leadership Traits in Administration

The teacher leader as Detective understands it is difficult for a school to meet its objectives when the principal is unsuccessful. In an era when principals often enter the job with little or no administrative experience, teacher leaders will need to stand ready to support them as they explore their own leadership strengths and abilities. The Detective is often the one who can help a principal recognize a particular strength or offer support in identifying and responding to what could be a blind spot in his or her leadership capacities. This leads to a more caring, supportive, and learner-centered environment for everyone to work and the Detective helps make that climate possible.

They Identify Strengths and Abilities Within the Community

As teacher leaders mature and evolve, they develop the capacity to exert influence from the classroom, throughout their school, and ultimately to the community and beyond (Crowther, Kaagan, Ferguson, & Hann, 2002). When teacher leaders as Detectives evolve, they develop the capacity to help the community identify the genius that lies within their city limits and capitalize on that discovery not only to add value to the school, but also to the community.

While these may seem to be lofty goals for teachers struggling to make a difference for the students they serve, there is a hand-in-glove fit to reaching out to the community and gaining support for the work being completed in the school. When the community realizes how much can be done for the school, collective capacity increases, and the school receives new levels of support that accelerate its efforts.

Looking in the Mirror: Becoming the Detective

We would like you to once again consider your existing mental models as they relate to the teacher leader as Detective. Try to evaluate your teaching practice according to this scale quickly without analyzing it too deeply. This will provide you an honest look at yourself in relation to this type of teacher leadership.

Discussion of Classroom Applications

Not unlike their law-enforcement counterparts, Detectives get better with time and practice at identifying learning challenges and responding to these challenges as needed. Professional learning communities and virtual networks help break down the isolation teachers have experienced in the past. Now that many schools have taken steps to work together, teacher leaders as Detectives can help each other identify strengths and capitalize on them for continuous improvement.

Discussion of Schoolwide Change

The reason CEOs are paid so highly is not that they can follow a preset script. We tend to reward leaders who can identify

Classroom Applications for the Detective

Old Reflection		*New Reflection*
The students go to the teacher to learn and, we hope, find their gifts.	5 4 3 2 1 0 1 2 3 4 5 ◄——►	The teacher goes to the students and looks for greatness not yet discovered and seeks to share that discovery.
Homework is primarily an exercise to measure the student's dedication and willingness to follow teacher's orders.	5 4 3 2 1 0 1 2 3 4 5 ◄——►	Homework is a mechanism to uncover clues in regard to learning hindrances and potential gifts the student may possess.
Teachers toil in isolation in attempting to understand the learning challenges of their students and the steps they can take in finding resolutions.	5 4 3 2 1 0 1 2 3 4 5 ◄——►	Teachers participate in numerous face-to-face and virtual learning spaces designed to provide mutual levels of support in understanding student learning challenges and identifying opportunities to respond and improve instructional performance.

unique strengths in an organization and capitalize on them in a way that adds value for everyone. Even successful CEOs moving from one organization to another won't necessarily lead change in exactly the same way. They realize that different circumstances require different approaches. Using the Detective's capacity to identify strengths and to build expectations, teacher leaders can lead change by responding with great dexterity when they discover skills and abilities in others.

Schoolwide Change for the Detective

Old Reflection		*New Reflection*
With highly evolved skills of detection, the teacher observes the faults of the principal and calls those faults out with his colleagues.	5 4 3 2 1 0 1 2 3 4 5 ←——→	With highly evolved skills of detection, the teacher observes the strengths of the principal and attempts to collaborate with others to enhance them.
The work of the teacher is driven primarily by job description, contract status, and local building practice.	5 4 3 2 1 0 1 2 3 4 5 ←——→	The work of the teacher is continually reinvented based on the strengths and gifts that are discovered, nurtured, and expanded upon.
Schools attempt to employ a narrowly defined, prepackaged process for facilitating school improvement.	5 4 3 2 1 0 1 2 3 4 5 ←——→	Schools personalize their approach to school improvement based on the unique strengths and emerging capabilities of the staff in the school.

Strategies for Becoming and Supporting the Detective

Ken Bishop, a longtime superintendent, told us that one of the most important things a leader can do is realize that you can't wait for the perfect opportunity to lead change. Waiting for that magic moment when certain individuals leave or retire, or planning on some momentous change once new individuals are hired, can often result in frustration.

While it's true that having the right people in the right positions makes a huge difference in long-term progress, Ken's message was that there is no substitute for going as far as you can with the team you have. Waiting to take action in the hope that a change in personnel will make a difference isn't as profitable as maximizing the individual and collective strengths available.

Schools that have succeeded in driving significant levels of change make these improvements by unearthing unique passions, skills, competencies, and perspectives among current staff. In this section, we will explore strategies for helping individuals and teams get to know the Detective perspective and build a school culture where discoveries and revelations happen consistently.

Hidden Strengths Strategy

You have undoubtedly heard the phrase, "You don't know your own strength." While most of the time this refers to some physical act, it is true that in many cases we don't see ourselves as clearly as we should. We are equipped with strengths and abilities that we either don't realize or aren't confident enough in to explore and express. One of the most powerful things a team can do to maximize its capacities and unearth hidden abilities is to have a hidden-talents discussion.

The size of the team will dictate to some degree how this discussion is held. A moderately sized team somewhat acquainted with one another may already devote some time to exploring the strengths of individual members. This is a radical departure from the deficit model that most of us work from, so the conversation alone will create a stimulating environment. When coming together and devoting time to the exploration of each teammate's talents, the team will become closer and connect with each other in new ways.

When participating in such a conversation, the team member being examined almost always learns new things. While these conversations have to be handled with care, they invariably result in the identification of talents and abilities in each person that they didn't know they had or didn't realize others noticed. Conducting this kind of discussion annually will help each team member understand what others see in them and how they can continue to explore their gifts and make a better contribution.

Another powerful aspect of this strategy involves the identification of team strengths and the unique benefits the individuals generate by working together. Put another way, what does the fusing of these individual talents create? Given all the abilities at the table, what capacities does the team have?

The team may realize that thanks to the patience and efficiency of several team members, combined with the passion and strategic thinking of several others, along with the wit and creativity of yet another, this group is able to stay motivated, look at problems in a unique way, and resist the emotional roller coaster that often comes with deep levels of change. By working together, such a group of very different individuals creates a new level of effectiveness and improves their output.

Thus, the exploration of teacher leadership from a Detective's perspective helps identify those team attributes that emerge when certain individuals come together and discover their combined capacity to make a difference.

Question What You See Strategy

Good detectives don't take things at face value. A first look at a crime scene may not say anything about what actually happened. The teacher leader as Detective will not be fooled by a first impression or initial conclusion. Instead, they reflect carefully on what they observe and formulate perceptions based on thoughtful consideration of the variables involved.

They are careful to not allow emotions to overwhelm their powers of perception. In good times or bad, they are always looking for the essence of the situation to better understand what is happening and to more adroitly identify the actions that need to be taken in the future to improve learning.

Genius Pursuit Strategy

The driving belief of the teacher leader as Detective is that there is untapped genius in everyone. They believe teacher teams and schools can find these attributes under the right circumstances and it is the Detective's mission to make this happen.

At the heart of this sensibility is a powerful belief in human beings. If we enter the teaching profession believing that only a select few have the capacity to lead and are smart enough to innovate, grow, and evolve, we will likely be disappointed throughout most of our careers. Simply waiting for genius to arrive, especially in teaching, minimizes the opportunities we share to find unlocked potential within ourselves and within our colleagues. Detectives believe that genius is waiting to be discovered just around the corner.

Just as the role of the Servant teacher leader is to seek out goodness in others, the role of the Detective is to seek out genius. The Detective knows that a transcendent thought might never be released unless individuals are sure that this type of input is, in fact, desired within the organization.

Detectives know it is counterproductive to view classrooms filled with students as just another stereotypical group of kids. In every class we teach, there may be students with the potential to change the world, perhaps due in some measure to the genius that lies within.

Pattern Examination Strategy

The Detective knows that individuals gradually reveal themselves at almost every turn. A student who is frustrated by an inability to keep up with classmates academically will demonstrate that frustration in any number of ways. The student may lash out at classmates, interrupt the teacher, or create disruptions in class.

A teacher leader may notice these negative patterns of behavior and seek to interrupt them, not for ensuring compliance or obedience in the class, but to meet the student's need to keep pace academically and feel more comfortable with his or her peers.

It may take time for the Detective to determine when to embrace or interrupt the patterns they observe. What is important is that they never stop looking for clues that lead to the true meaning of these patterns.

Uncomfortable Observation Strategy

One of the patterns teacher leaders as Detectives may notice in their schools is an obsession with vacations. There may be signs counting down to Christmas or spring break or summer vacation. There may even be weekly countdowns to the bell ringing Friday afternoon signaling that teachers and students are free to enjoy the weekend. Detectives may observe that conversations in the teachers' lounge revolve around how many years certain teachers have until retirement.

While this pattern may seem innocent, the Detective notices that these seemingly playful countdowns send a message that everyone in the school, including the teachers and principals, is anxious to be free of teaching and learning. Treating each week, year, or career like a prison sentence slowly being counted down in anticipation of freedom may seem fun, but the Detective will challenge his or her team to consider the implications of the message being sent.

Persistence Strategy

The teacher leader as Detective acknowledges that in many situations, the case may never be solved. This doesn't have to result in frustration. The Detective has learned to contend with this sense of continuousness. He or she recognizes that as soon as a situation seems to be resolved, new variables emerge that require reevaluation and a possible adjustment in approach.

These changing circumstances will leave new clues for the Detective to pursue, invariably opening new chapters for growth and improvement along the way. The willingness to persist and stay open to new evidence keeps teaching interesting and helps open the door for new opportunities.

Positive Choice Strategy

The field of psychology has brought focus in recent years to the power of positive choice. Positive psychology advocates refocusing our mental energies away from negative memories or thought patterns and switching to positive habits for a more affirming vision of the future (Barnett, 2006; Friedel, Cortina, Turner, & Midgley, 2007; Lazarus, 1998). This is a direct contradiction to previously held assumptions about human behavior wherein the focus was on a debilitating problem or concern, rather than a new goal or aspiration.

From a psychological standpoint, the notion that improvements can be gleaned by focusing on positive goals and aspirations should bring new attention to the importance of maintaining an optimistic outlook. If psychologists are finding that human beings respond well to this system, it seems fitting that teacher leaders would likewise consider the power of positive choice when leading change.

You may have a long-held personal belief that focusing on the negativity of the past seems to bring little value to any school improvement initiative. Today, a body of research is being developed that would support the notion that a better outcome, individually or collectively, is likely to emerge by choosing to identify a positive, empowering, and improved outcome to work toward in the future.

The teacher leader as Detective should immerse him- or herself in the pursuit of what's possible, what's right, and what's good. This doesn't mean that teacher leaders as Detectives become motivational speakers looking for the next sunny day. Instead, they are the Detectives who look for the clues to unlock the mystery of a better, more impactful, and empowering future for the school.

Positive Deviance Strategy

The concept of positive deviance arose in the 1970s, when aid workers realized their strategies for helping impoverished villages in third-world countries were not yielding the improvement they had hoped for. Several creative workers suggested studying village outliers, whose ability to raise food was significantly above the norm. It was postulated that the practices used in the successful outliers could be applied in other villages.

In testing this assumption, the aid workers found that even though the challenges from one village to the next might be very different, given the topography and other local hindrances that could exist, there were almost always individuals in the village who were outperforming their counterparts. By simply identifying these positive outliers and encouraging them to share their knowledge, the villages found new levels of prosperity. While this seems like a common-sense solution, remember that it took the support of outsiders to work with the villagers to help them share the answers they had already discovered.

Over the years, scholars have studied the implications of this assumption. Today, leadership and organizational development theorists encourage leaders at all levels to consider the advantages of identifying successful performers who deviate from the norm both in their strategies and in the results they realize (Marsh, Schroeder, Dearden, Sternin, & Sternin, 2000).

This leadership concept can be of great value if applied consistently in P–12 education, especially when led by teacher leaders. Even the most progressive principals often find themselves so busy that they fail to recognize deep and profound levels of classroom innovation occurring in their school.

Often, teachers who have been innovative in their approaches to working with students have done so in relative isolation. They haven't had the opportunity to share their ideas and practices. The teacher leader as Detective identifies these positive deviations and encourages the exploration of their approaches.

Hidden Treasure Strategy

Stories make a difference. Every school contains stories of excellence and how teachers' gifts led them to new heights in service and support. To help support the ongoing detection of strengths and abilities, it is helpful to publicly call out moments of brilliance when a teacher finds his or her own unique strengths. This is also a good time to publicly acknowledge the Detective who spotted the talented teacher. It may also inspire more Detectives to emerge in the school.

TRANSCENDENT TEACHER LEADERS IN ACTION: THE DETECTIVE

The exemplary teacher leaders featured in Chapter 1 consistently detected truth, goodness, and possibility in those around them. Kate didn't see a classroom full of recalcitrant teens. She saw emerging college students. Year after year, Mary Ann was given a full slate of students in a tough, urban school who perhaps were unsuccessful and uninterested in math. In them, she saw a capacity to form a cooperative group that would work well together and exceed the expectations of almost everyone. Time and time again, Jim looked into the hearts and minds of the players he coached and saw untapped potential and excellence. Like a true Detective, he identified the glimpses of greatness he noticed and cleared the pathway they could follow to display those gifts.

How many gifts, talents, and abilities go unrecognized in your school each year? How many students have some secret capacity that they don't even know about that could emerge under the right circumstances? How many teachers in your school are capable of transcendent outcomes like those described in this book, but somehow have yet to marshal the strength, courage, or focus to bring those talents forward? Could you be the Detective who helps transform your school by identifying gifts and talents in others and helping each individual develop those talents? How different would your school be if there were numerous Detectives at work, enriching the climate each year with new discoveries? How rich could your school be if these talents and treasures were revealed?

Conclusions

Being a teacher leader who seeks out strengths and talents in others is an empowering model for how teachers can lead and influence change in their school. Unfortunately, the images of teaching have at times run in complete contradiction to this new image of teacher leadership. Consider the old mental model where students were seen as empty vessels that approached the fountain of knowledge with humble appreciation, waiting to be filled with new understanding. This image of learning held onto the hope that benevolent masters would generously share their knowledge.

On your first day of teaching, you probably didn't see yourself as a super sleuth cracking the case of greatness in others. We challenge you to look into the mirror and see the possibilities that could emerge if teacher leadership included a strong and dedicated focus on detecting the strengths of others and using this ability to lead the way.

We hope that this magnifying glass communicates how Detectives are always looking more deeply than others at the world around them. That's the way Detectives notice clues that may go unnoticed. We hope that you keep this symbol in mind when faced with those moments when it's time to seek and draw out untold greatness in others.

Conclusion

Through our father-and-son writing effort, we have shared many decades of experience in reflecting on teaching. We have seen and experienced changes in the profession. We remain inspired and optimistic about the future. Thomas Friedman (2005) famously referred to technology's flattening force on the world, where the walls come down and traditions and conventions are reexamined. Technology is changing our profession. Many of the limiting conventions from the past are gone and we believe teacher leadership can bridge the gap as these hindrances fade away.

We will need **Learning Advocates** to keep a focus on the latest learning research. The **Believer** will inspire us with hope and keep us from dwelling in negative spaces that prevent us from becoming our inspired best.

While most of us strive to improve, the **Transformationalist** will seek better outcomes than any of us could have imagined. The **Synergizer** will keep us connected and show us new worlds of collaboration. **Method Masters** will hone their craft and yield breakthroughs that will reshape our change expectations. We will feel grounded, at home, and ready to learn with the influence of the **Fully Invested Owner.** The **Present Balance Keeper** will inspire us to act now, and to be patient when at first we don't succeed.

The **Servant** won't let us forget what we work for and the **Inquisitor** will help keep us energized, while questioning our methods, our goals, and ourselves. The **Detective** will help us find those hidden gifts within one another.

The good news is that all of these models of teacher leadership are available to you right now. They're free, and they're more powerful than anything else in education. Teacher leadership is growing more important in schools, not just for teachers, but for the administration that supports them. In fact, principals with a teacher-leadership orientation were found to be significantly more transformational in their leadership style (Reason, 2006).

The next time a teacher or a principal tells you something can't be done, compare the challenge to building a school for girls under the watchful eye of the Taliban. Anything is possible. Think about the four teacher leaders we profiled in this book. You could put them in a professional learning community or on the moon. Just give them students and great things will happen.

Imagine a school full of teachers like Mary Ann, Jim, Kate, and Khris. What if more and more teacher leaders like these four got busy and decided to create deeper levels of change? The examples provided in Chapter 1 clearly point out that you don't have to be exceptional to be a teacher leader. You simple have to demonstrate an exceptional desire to affect change and maintain a belief that this type of change is possible. To the present and future teacher leaders reading this book, we invite you to get determined. Stay open to possibility and spend your days seeking greatness in others, and in yourself. Now you're ready. Go out there and lead!

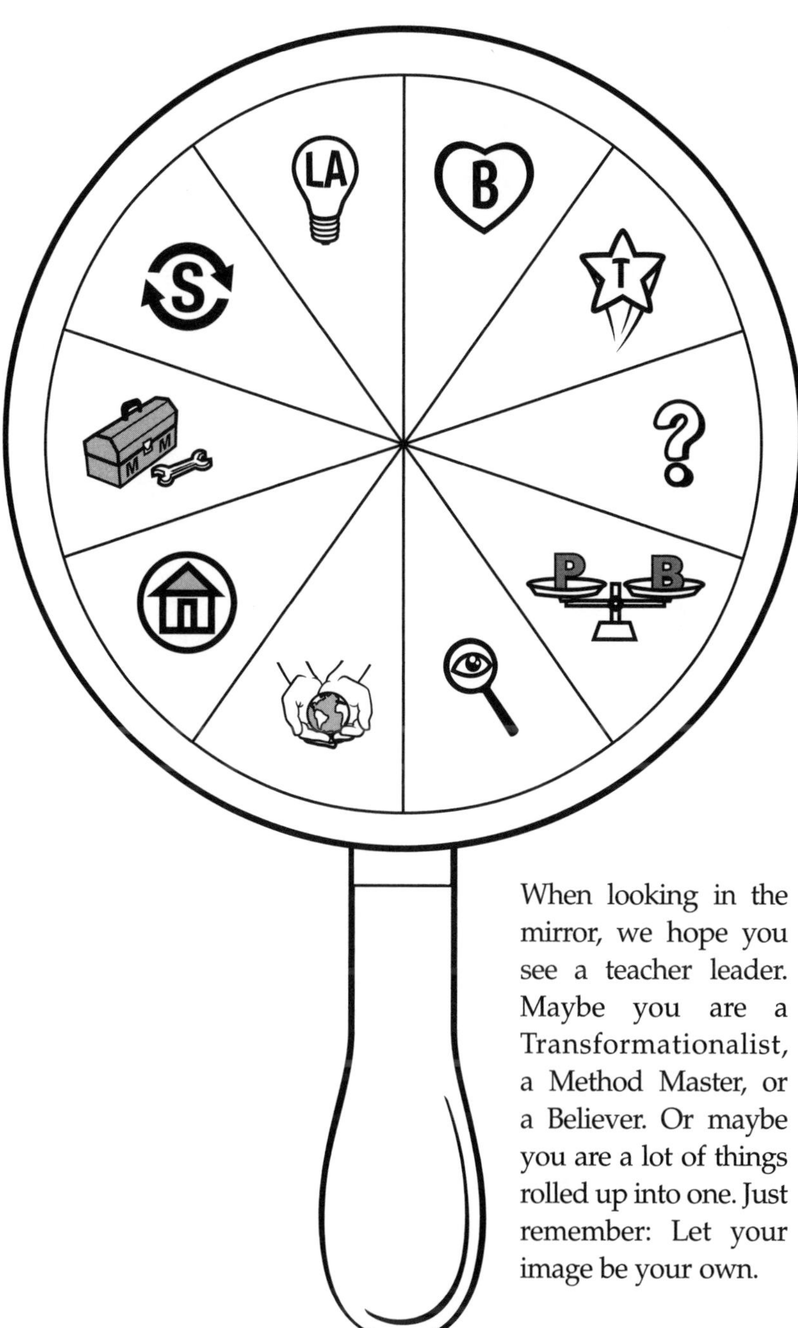

When looking in the mirror, we hope you see a teacher leader. Maybe you are a Transformationalist, a Method Master, or a Believer. Or maybe you are a lot of things rolled up into one. Just remember: Let your image be your own.

References

Achterman, D., & Loertscher, D. V. (2008). Where in the role are you anyway? *CSLA Journal, 31*(2), 10–13.

Armantier, O. (2004). Does observation influence learning? *Games and Economic Behavior, 46*, 221–239.

Bapuji, H., & Crossan, M. (2004). From questions to answers: Reviewing organizational learning research. *Management Learning, 35*(4), 397–417.

Barnett, M. M. (2006). Does it hurt to know the worst? Psychological morbidity, information preferences and understanding of prognosis in patients with advanced cancer. *Psycho-Oncology, 15*(1), 44–55.

Bernhardt, V. L. (2009). *Data, data everywhere: Bringing all the data together for continuous school improvement.* Larchmont, NY: Eye on Education.

Blanchard, K. (1983). *The one minute manager.* New York: Berkley Trade.

Blanchard, K. (2009). *Leading at a higher level: Blanchard on leadership and creating high-performing organizations.* Upper Saddle River, NJ: FT Press.

Bonk, C. J. (2009). *The world is open: How web technology is revolutionizing education.* San Francisco: Jossey-Bass.

Bonnema, T. R. (2009). *Enhancing student learning with brain-based research.* (ERIC Document Reproduction Service No. ED510039)

Braine, M. E. (2009). The role of the hypothalamus: Part 1. The regulation of temperature and hunger. *British Journal of Neuroscience Nursing, 5*(2), 66–72.

Caine, R. N., Caine, G., McClintic, C., & Klimek, K. (2005). *12 brain/mind learning principles in action.* Thousand Oaks, CA: Corwin.

Chapman, C., Ramondt, L., & Smiley, G. (2005). Strong community, deep learning: Exploring the link. *Innovations in Education and Teaching International, 42*(3), 217–230.

Chen, G., Tjosvold, D., & Liu, C. (2006). Cooperative goals, leader people and productivity values: Their contribution to top management teams in China. *Journal of Management Studies, 43*(5), 1177–1200.

Childs, L. (2005, Spring). Creating a Galilean leadership shift. *National Staff Development Council, 26*(2), 22–26.

Clotfelter, C. T., Ladd, H. F., & Vigdor, J. L. (2007, January). *How and why do teacher credentials matter for student achievement?* (NBER Working Paper No. 12828). Cambridge, MA: National Bureau of Economic Research.

Cohen, D. A., & Robertson, E. M. (2007). Motor sequence consolidation: Constrained by critical time windows or competing components. *Experimental Brain Research, 177*(4), 440–446.

Compton, R. J. (2003). The interface between emotion and attention: A review of evidence from psychology and neuroscience. *Behavioral and Cognitive Neuroscience, 2*, 115–129.

Conger, J. A. (1989). Leadership: The art of empowering others. *The Academy of Management Executive, 3*(1), 17–24.

Cotman, C. W., & Engessar-Cesar, C. (2003). Exercise enhances and protects brain function. *Exercise & Sport Sciences Reviews, 30*(2), 75–79.

Coulter, C. M. (2006). Appreciating the best of our past to navigate the future. In *Currents and convergence: Navigating the rivers of change* (pp. 26–31). Paper presented at the twelfth national conference of the Association of College and Research Libraries, Minneapolis, MN.

Crowther, F. (with Ferguson, M., & Hann, L.). (2008). *How teacher leadership enhances school success* (2nd ed.). Thousand Oaks, CA: Corwin.

Crowther, F., Kaagan, S. S., Ferguson, M., & Hann, L. (2002). *Developing teacher leaders: How teacher leadership enhances school success.* Thousand Oaks, CA: Corwin.

Daggett, W. R. (2000). Moving from standards to instructional practice. *National Association of Secondary School Principals, 84*(620), 66–72.

DuFour, R. (2004). What is a professional learning community? *Educational Leadership, 61*(8), 6–11.

DuFour, R., Eaker, R., & DuFour, R. (2008). *Revisiting professional learning communities at work: New insights for improving schools.* Bloomington, IN: Solution Tree.

Egorov, A. V., Unsicker, K., & von Bohlen, O. (2006). Muscarinic control of graded persistent activity in lateral amygdale neurons. *European Journal of Neuroscience, 24*(11), 3183–3194.

Eisner, E. W. (2002). *The educational imagination.* Columbus, OH: Prentice Hall.

Friedel, K. S., Cortina, J., Turner, C., & Midgley, C. (2007). Achievement goals, efficacy beliefs and coping strategies in mathematics: The roles of perceived parent and teacher goal emphases. *Contemporary Educational Psychology, 32*(3), 434–458.

Friedman, T. (2005). *The world is flat: A brief history of the twenty-first century.* New York: Farrar, Straus and Giroux.

Fullan, M. (2001). *The new meaning of educational change.* New York: Teachers College Press.

George, P. S. (2005). A rationale for differentiating instruction in the regular classroom. *Theory Into Practice, 44*(3), 185–193.

Gray, K. (1993). Why we will lose: Taylorism in America's high schools. *Phi Delta Kappan, 74*(5), 370–375.

Greenleaf, R. K. (1970). *The servant as leader.* San Francisco: Jossey-Bass.

Harackiewicz, J. M., Barron, K. E., Tauer, J. M., Carter, S. M., & Elliot, A. J. (2000). Short-term and long-term consequences of achievement goals: Predicting interest and performance over time. *Journal of Educational Psychology, 92*(2), 316–330.

Janis, I. L. (1982). *Groupthink: Psychological studies of policy decisions and fiascoes.* Boston: Houghton Mifflin.

Johnson, B. (2003). Teacher collaboration: Good for some, not so good for others. *Educational Studies, 29*(4).

Jones, O. (2000). Scientific management, culture and control: A firsthand account of Taylorism in practice. *Human Relations, 53*(5), 631–653.

Katzenmeyer, M., & Moller, G. (2001). *Awakening the sleeping giant* (2nd ed.). Thousand Oaks, CA: Corwin.

Koenig, S., & Mecklinger, A. (2008). Electrophysiological correlates of encoding and retrieving emotional events. *Emotion, 8*(2), 162–173.

Lazarus, R. (1998). The costs and benefits of denial. In R. S. Lazarus (Ed.), *Fifty years of research and theory* (pp. 227–251). Mahwah, NJ: Lawrence Erlbaum.

Lee, D., & Birdsong Sabatino, K. (1998). Evaluating guided reflection: A U.S. case study. *International Journal of Training and Development, 2*(3), 162–170.

Leithwood, K. (1995). *Effective school district leadership: Transforming politics into education.* New York: SUNY Press.

Levenson, R. W. (2003). Autonomic specificity and emotion. In R. J. Davidson, H. H. Goldsmith, & K. R. Scherer (Eds.), *Handbook of effective science* (pp. 212–224). New York: Oxford University Press.

Lieberman, A., & Miller, L. (2005). Teachers as leaders. *The Educational Forum, 69*(2), 151–161.

Marsh, D. R., Schroeder, D. G., Dearden, K. A., Sternin, J., & Sternin, M. (2000). The power of positive deviance. *BMJ, 329,* 1177–1179.

Martin, N. K., & Shoho, A. R. (2000, January 27–29). *Teacher experience, training, & age: The influence of teacher characteristics on classroom management style.* Paper presented at the annual meeting of the Southwest Educational Research Association, Dallas, TX.

Martin, T., McCrone, S., Bower, M., & Dindyal, J. (2005). The interplay of teacher and student actions in the teaching and learning of geometric proof. *Educational Studies in Mathematics, 60*(1), 95–124.

Mayers, R. S., & Zapeda, S. J. (2002). High school department chairs: Role ambiguity and conflict during change. *NASSP Bulletin, 86*(632), 49–64.

Merrill, M. D., & Gilbert, C. G. (2008). Effective peer interaction in a problem-centered instructional strategy. *Distance Education, 29*(2), 199–207.

Nolen-Hoeksema, S. (1991). Responses to depression and their effects on the duration of depressive episodes. *Journal of Abnormal Psychology, 100*, 569–582.

O'Reilly, R. C., & Frank, M. J. (2006). Making working memory work: A computational model of learning in the prefrontal cortex and basal ganglia. *Neural Computation, 18*(2), 283–328.

Patterson, J., & Patterson, J. (2004, April). Sharing the lead. *Educational Leadership, 61*(7), 74–78.

Pekrun, R., Maier, M., & Elliot, A. (2009). Achievement goals and achievement emotions: Testing a model of their joint relations with academic performance. *Journal of Education Psychology, 101*(1), 115–135.

Reason, C. (2010). *Leading a learning organization: The science of working with others.* Bloomington, IN: Solution Tree.

Reason, L. D. (2006). *An investigation of the relationship between transformational and transactional principal leadership behaviors and an orientation in teacher leadership.* Unpublished doctoral dissertation, Capella University.

Smith-Burke, M. T. (1996). Professional development for teacher leaders: Promoting program ownership and increased success. *Network News*, pp. 1–4.

Srivastava, A., Bartol, K. M., & Locke, E. A. (2006). Empowering leadership in management teams: Effects on knowledge sharing, efficacy, and performance. *Academy of Management Journal, 49*(6), 1239–1251.

Stout, M. (2006). *The paranoia switch: How terror rewires our brains and reshapes our behavior and how we can reclaim our courage.* New York: Sarah Crichton.

Wood, G. E., Norris, E. H., Waters, E., & Stoldt, J. (2008). Chronic immobilization stress alters aspects of emotionality and associative learning in the rat. *Behavioral Neuroscience, 122*(2), 282–292.

Zorn, T. E., Page, D. J., & Cheney, G. (2000). Nuts about change: Multiple perspectives on change-oriented communication in a public sector organization. *Management Communication Quarterly, 13*(4), 515–566.

Index